Highlighting Homeschooling

Highlighting Homeschooling

Bethany M. Gardiner, M.D.

**sticky
tape
press**

Provo, Utah

© Copyright 2010 by Bethany Gardiner

ISBN 978-0-9830420-0-6

Cover art: Lucas Gibson

Library of Congress Control Number: 2010914140

98765432 First Printing

Sticky Tape Press
1458 E 330 N. Provo, UT 84606
www.stickytapepress.com

To Dad, who taught me how to reach for the stars while keeping my feet firmly planted on the ground.

Contents

Acknowledgements

Highlighting Homeschooling would not have been possible without the help of so many people that gave me their time, friendship, and support. I would like to thank all the intrepid homeschooling families that I have met. They have shared their stories, both the successes and failures, and have helped me follow in their footsteps. Without the support and guidance of fellow homeschoolers, I don't know how I could have continued on my own homeschooling journey. I would also like to thank my family. My children patiently allowed me to test out my theories on them and my wonderful husband was always there for me during the process of creating this book. In addition, my editors, Matt and Linda, and my graphic designer, Luke, have been instrumental in helping me take my ideas and turn them into this project. To everyone who helped turn this dream into a reality – thanks.

Introduction

Most of the available information about homeschooling deals with the educational aspect alone, but a complete discussion of homeschooling can't happen without considering the lifestyle of your family as a whole. This is a familiar concept to me both as a homeschooling mother and as a pediatrician, a profession that requires doctors to work with entire families to improve children's health. Because homeschooling takes place in the home (in its broadest definition), which is the center of family life, to talk about it without considering the whole family is really an injustice.

No two children, families, or situations are exactly the same and because homeschoolers are so diverse, it isn't possible to cover every situation concerning homeschooling. However, there are many important aspects that are universally applicable and I've selected some of these to discuss.

This book explores some of the choices available to homeschoolers and potential homeschoolers and lays out the benefits and pitfalls of the homeschooling lifestyle, all with two goals. First, I want to highlight some issues that often aren't addressed adequately in the homeschooling community, such as socialization, planning, finding materials, and keeping your sanity while homeschooling. There are also issues that arise from having your children at home all the time that are hard to adjust to, such as how to get your house clean, run errands, and find time for yourself. Homeschooling parents need to figure out their inspirations and motivations for taking on this responsibility and learn how to continue to meet their own needs while simultaneously meeting those of their family. The successful homeschooling family needs to develop flexibility and adaptability while still focusing an uncompromising eye on their goals.

Second, I want to explore the benefits of individualized education. Modern education touts a homogenized, one-size-fits-all mentality that doesn't allow children to rise to their individual potentials. Homeschooling can help families move away from this narrow outlook both in education and in life, allowing for more varied experiences and expressions of individuality. Individuality is to be celebrated. It's what makes us human, capable of innovation and progress. Let's promote this from the outset with our children and our families.

The principles laid out in *Highlighting Homeschooling* are relevant for all families, no matter what the stage their children are at or where they are currently in the journey of homeschooling. Families with very small children, even infants, can incorporate these homeschooling principles into their life even before formal education begins. Families with school-age children that are investigating homeschooling or are partially supplementing their children's education can incorporate the principles spelled out here. Families that are already homeschooling will benefit from a refresher and an influx of new ideas.

There is much to explore with homeschooling, from the educational aspects to lifestyle changes to the positive impacts on families. I hope to show you that homeschooling is relevant and appropriate for all children, whether in totality or a supplement.

PART 1:
Highlighting the Basics

1

What *Is* Homeschooling, Anyway?

When I started writing this book, the spellchecker on my computer didn't recognize "homeschooling" as a word. I added it to the computer's lexicon, but not before I suffered a mini-crisis – was it actually two words? Maybe with a hyphen? Or (horrors) maybe the computer was right and it wasn't a word at all.

Not long ago, I was flipping through a dictionary and helping my son with a lesson when I got the urge to look up "homeschooling" and settle the matter once and for all. I found it on page 683, right between "homerun" and "homesick." Tiny as it is, this is the kind of sign that homeschoolers search for and celebrate, the kind that shows that homeschooling is becoming more popular. Parents of the estimated 2 million children that are currently being homeschooled in America still have to fight against entrenched ideas of institutionalized education to find what's right for our children; families that choose to homeschool their children are still a tiny minority compared to the approximately 50 million that are being traditionally schooled.

The definition that I was so excited to find in the dictionary sounded simple and straightforward: Homeschooling is "the fact or process of teaching one's children in the home instead of sending them to a school." I laughed to myself after reading it – things are never as easy as they sound.

Most species with babies that need to be nurtured after birth are taught the necessary survival skills by their parents. Without that parent-child teaching, the survival of the offspring is in serious danger. Western society, as it has become civilized and modern, has controverted this natural tendency in favor of segregating its smallest citizens into schools and outsourcing their teaching away from their parents. This process broadcasts the subconscious message that parents are either unable or unwilling to teach their children themselves. Homeschoolers resist this message and push on accepted norms, and in doing so carve out new niches for their families.

In today's society, where our life is technologically influenced to a great deal already, it's even more important to stress this interdependence and integration at home. As much as it would soothe parents to be able to box up education and send it off for someone else to deal with between the hours of nine a.m. and three p.m., it doesn't happen that way. Education is intertwined with the rest of life in a confusing array, a multi-tasker's paradise. But remember, by its very nature homeschooling integrates life into education and starts you down this road without any extra effort.

 HOMESCHOOLING HIGHLIGHT

Education shouldn't be compartmentalized away from daily life. It coexists and is intertwined with life and family. Homeschooling seamlessly integrates life and education.

So what is homeschooling, anyway? Simply put, homeschooling is educating your child in your home or other nontraditional environment.

It is as diverse as the many different ways you can think of to educate your child out of the typical classroom environment of a public or private school.

Who Homeschools?

Homeschoolers are hard to characterize as a group because of the diversity that brings families to homeschooling. Many paths lead parents to homeschooling, each with their own unique needs and methods. There are families with children in school that have found the traditional school model does not meet the needs of their children academically, socially, or both. There are families that have lifestyle constraints such as frequent or long-term travel that turn to homeschooling for its flexibility. There are also children who have talents in the arts or sports whose practice schedules don't mesh with traditional schools. And still yet, there are families that are dealing with special needs and illness, either chronic or acute, that are better served by homeschooling. Whatever factors lead parents to question the traditional school model accepted in society today, the inherent diversity that leads to this point calls for solutions that are just as diverse. Homeschooling celebrates this diversity and helps families create individual solutions for the individual needs of their children and families.

In writing this book, I wanted to create a work that helps parents find their own way. For families considering homeschooling as an option for their family, it's critical to be able to look at issues without being pressured to get things "right." Unfortunately, early on in my homeschooling adventure, I spent a considerable amount of effort trying to fit into molds created by others and ending up frustrated when they didn't work for my family. I worried when I read about "unschooling"[1] styles that I was too rigid. When I read about school-at-home techniques, I worried that I was too permissive. When I read a book on the Charlotte Mason[2] techniques, I worried that we didn't spend enough time outside writing nature journals. I eventually discovered that what I should have been worried about was nothing more than a simple question: Is what we're doing working for my children?

Early on, I thought that the homeschooling method I chose had to be concrete and all-encompassing. I've subsequently learned that in successful families, nothing is further from the truth. Sure, choosing a single method and sticking with it works for some families, but the majority of us use a combination of methods and approaches. As a result, I've tailored the premises of this book so they can be applied to any homeschooling style, from the most rigid school-at-home to the most child-led unschoolers.

Why Homeschool?

While the number of children in the public school system makes the number of homeschooled children look tiny, homeschooling is, in fact, the fastest growing educational trend in America, and both establishments and individuals are adapting to accommodate the change. Many noted universities are offering online courses for younger students, and many high schools are adopting "virtual school" models which increase the options for education in the home. While many of these changes aren't traditionally considered homeschooling, they represent the growing desire for customized education.

The core goal of the homeschooling movement is to improve the education of our children. Of course this refers to the "book learning" part of education – learning to read or do long division, for example – but it also refers to something more. Once you delve into the many choices available for teaching, it will become apparent that the decisions you make will have results extending far beyond the standard meaning of education. How you homeschool will have a far-reaching influence on the entire lifestyle of your family through the modeling that occurs as a natural complement to the one-on-one book learning of homeschooling. Some people refer to this as "character education," a nebulous phrase that covers values and morals, family customs, religious faith, work ethic, basic financial knowledge, and personal habits, to name a few topics.

Oops – I mentioned religion. At this point, I'm sure that some reading this are throwing up their hands and saying, "Here we go, another zealot's morality lecture!" Probably there are others who are worried that this book is for "those secular types" because that mention wasn't on page one. You can all rest easy, because one topic that you won't find in this book is religion. Besides being a very personal and emotional subject, I honestly don't find it relevant to many of the topics discussed in this book.

I've been privileged over my years of homeschooling to meet people from different faiths and many degrees of involvement in those faiths. While these beliefs will certainly guide an individual's choice of curriculum and extracurricular activities, I've found the items included in this book were topics of conversation or were observations I found in all groups I associated with. No matter what religious philosophy you subscribe to, your children and their education are at the forefront of all you do, and the unique situation of educating your children at home brings on issues we have in common regardless of religious persuasion.

Every parent concerns themselves with providing their children the tools to achieve a successful and happy life. However, what exactly constitutes success and how does one achieve it? How can you be sure your children are getting the necessary instruction to meet all of their future needs? What are the components of a well-rounded education beyond the "book-learning"? These life skills and character development pieces of education are often left out of a traditional school model, partially because they tend to cause a lot of controversy given the diversity of our culture.

In the past, it was assumed these skills were taught in the home. And while I believe this is the proper place for this type of education to take place, it's becoming harder to do so. There are many competing forces out there that can lure children away from the lessons taught at home. We have instant messaging, email, iPods, TiVo, and the internet, to name just a few examples. These are great ways to connect with the world at large but they also tend to erode family time.

HOMESCHOOLING HIGHLIGHT

Education has several components, not all derived from books. Home-schooling combines all of these components without any extra effort.

Unfortunately, through no fault of our own, many of us are finding the time to impart these character and life skills to our children shrinking fast. Parents are struggling for ways to regain a family-centric lifestyle without forsaking other interests or impacting the book learning they know is so important.

All elements of education, both book learning, character, and life skills, need to be taught and modeled in order for children to grow and find success and happiness in their lives. But actually doing this is a daunting task, one that parents struggle with on a daily basis. Home-schooling provides a place to start building a complete education from the ground up. The education of our children is integrated into every-day life, not sequestered in a separate brick and mortar edifice.

Even though to many the word "homeschooling" represents nothing more than a change of the location of the educative process, it really encompasses much more. The access you have to your children will allow you to seamlessly incorporate character education and life skills into your daily teaching. You can teach your children how to live while you teach everything else, without having to worry about unteaching anything taught by someone else. The lifestyle opened up to you with continual parent-child dialogue will force you to grow and change as you confront not only your own worries, but also outside influences and judgments.

🔺 In a conversation I had at a friend's house as our kids met for a play date, one mom spent a good five minutes bemoaning the problems she had teaching her daughter, and not surprisingly the conversation turned to parenting issues. One of the homeschooling parents was an accomplished birth coach and La Leche League leader. She said she wished there was a La Leche League for her ten year old, as she didn't feel nearly as confident as the parent of a tween. The help this group had provided to her while parenting a newborn was invaluable, and she wanted the same support as her child aged. We all laughed, but we also saw her point. She wanted a lifestyle prescription that would be all-encompassing. Looking at homeschooling as this type of solution can really change the way a family interacts. There is no need for you to separate being a parent with all of the attendant responsibilities of being a teacher and the education of your children.

As a pediatrician, when parents would bring their children to me with questions, they were often not really asking questions, but rather asking for affirmation that their choices were correct. It was rare that an answer was a definite yes or no, because often the answers were rooted in lifestyles, not rules. Of course there are the non-negotiables, like providing appropriate medical care, food, and shelter for your children and teaching them not to run into a street or get into vehicles with strangers. But the vast majority of parenting involves the negotiable items that live in individual comfort zones.

Can You Do It? Yes, of Course!

Even after hearing all of this, it's not unusual for people wondering about homeschooling to doubt that they can succeed. The idea of outsourcing education to an all-knowing school system is compelling. However, parents are too quick to sell themselves short. There's no one more concerned about the well-being and education of your children than you. No one will be more accountable for their future success than you. No one will be more flexible and adaptable to their needs than you. We should not have to abdicate control because we are told there's someone more capable out there.

I like to think of educating my children in terms of transportation. It's acceptable to get an assigned driver (public school) or hire a shuttle service (private school) to take them where they need to be. However, education doesn't have a pre-defined destination; the destination tends to depend on what the passengers see along the way. With someone else driving, it's difficult to take side trips or anticipate bumps in the road. Being in the driver's seat (homeschooling) is the best way to make sure your children get where they want to go.

Why are side trips so important? And why is it important for you to decide when and where they will occur? Their importance lies in the way that children learn. When new ideas are presented, it's vital to be able to expand on them and fit them into the larger context of what has already been learned. This happens in different ways for different learning styles. It also is important to be able to slow down, speed up, or even stop altogether, depending on the needs of the passengers. When you're in control, without having to justify your reasoning to another authority, the rough patches are much easier to navigate.

Even though we focus primarily on children when speaking about homeschooling, another essential part of the discussion of homeschooling needs to revolve around the parents engaged and committed to it. Getting inspired to make changes in the first place will translate to the motivation needed to continue the journey and finally into the confidence to overcome obstacles. I've learned that the only inspiration I'll ever get will come from within myself and my family. Finding your own source of confidence is very important to the homeschooling parent. It will help you get through tough dilemmas, bad days, and those times when you wish you could expel your children from their homeschool.

▲ As a pediatrician, I was trained not only to look after sick children, but also to look after the emotional and mental well-being of healthy children. Effectively dealing with these clinical needs required me to address the family's parenting style, interactions, work-life choices, and other parenting issues, from friends to schools to childcare. I was able to gain insight into the importance of individual variations in these decisions, and I quickly learned there was no magic recipe for success. I could advise, give guidelines, and be an advocate for the children, but the actual definitive answers had to come from within the family unit.

I learned something very important in my years of practice and that was how to listen to children, both verbally and non-verbally. Many times the clues to the problems families are having are right in front of them in their children, but they can't recognize them or they don't want to verbalize them. About ninety-five percent of the behavioral problems I evaluated stemmed from school and/or family life. The kids were over-scheduled, stressed out, suffering from peer pressure, lack of parental attention, illnesses from daycare, and the pressure of conforming inside the boxes of today's standards of acceptable practices.

When I started homeschooling, I realized that by its very nature, many of these concerns are erased. The connections between homeschooling and lifestyle are significant and far-reaching. I think this was the most attractive part of the homeschooling lifestyle for me; the family life produced by having the children at home is by necessity child-focused and individualized.

One place to develop confidence is in the process of taking control of your child's education. There are schoolteachers out there who go home frustrated because their classes aren't progressing or because they are falling behind schedule. The difference with homeschooling is that we have the ability to make time up. We can go back to a lesson in the evening, or on the weekend, or during vacation time, whereas schoolteachers cannot. If our child doesn't learn something the first time through, we can teach it again. We don't have to worry about completing a set amount of work in a set time and can tailor the learning to meet our expectations and those of our children instead of someone else.

The process of finding your inspiration isn't easy, but the hardships and uncertainties do have a balance. Today, just after I finished the laundry, fed the starving natives, and got the vocabulary lesson done, my daughter made an off-hand remark about how stupid the poem was that I had given her to read. It came out of her little mouth in such an indignant way, like she was astonished that anyone could have the temerity to waste her time like that. I started laughing, then the kids started, and soon the three of us were laughing so hard we were crying. That got us started on funny limericks and nonsensical rhymes, and we spent at least an hour composing funny poems. Her snark grew into a great deposit in the memory bank.

Everyone has moments when nothing seems to be going right. When you have just cleaned up all the art supplies and turn around to find them all out again in an even bigger state of disarray because one edge of the project didn't get its fair share of glitter glue, just take a deep breath. Every parent who has homeschooled has been there with you. These moments can be balanced against those proud parenting moments when your child meets a traditionally schooled child on the playground and tries to convince him or her to leave school because homeschooling is so great, or when adults comment about how polite, well-spoken, and confident your children are.

The philosophy behind homeschooling is deeper than the dictionary definition we started with. It comprises not just the location of schooling, but the attitudes surrounding the educational process. Education can be woven into the very fabric of life. Processes and methods are better when they are developed within the family rather than being imposed upon them. The very act of developing what works for you and your children will lead to the confidence needed to continue the process. Regardless of your place in the journey of homeschooling – at the beginning or in the thick of it – there's much to be learned by continually examining and tweaking your processes and methods. After all, education should be a dynamic life-long process, not a jail sentence.

2

Getting Started or Starting Fresh

I don't know exactly the first time we identified ourselves as a home-schooling family. It was more of a gradual movement into the position than a definite declaration. Looking back, I realize that we have been on journey as a family, with a lot of bumps and surprises along the way.

Like all parents, my husband and I want the best for our kids, and when they were young we thought that "the best" was found with a good nanny and plenty of ancillary help. My husband and I were busy with two full-time careers, I as a pediatrician and he as a finance executive for a large company. As my oldest child approached preschool age, we dutifully started to inspect the area preschools, sure that the right school was part of "the best" as well.

We finally found a Montessori preschool at a local church that was highly regarded and reasonably inexpensive. I was on maternity leave with my daughter at this time and was able to spend a lot of time at the preschool observing and getting familiar with the way the school worked. I was amazed at how much time was spent lining the children up to go places, or getting them quieted down for instruction. My son loved school and the kids and teachers were great, but he didn't learn one single thing in the two and a half months he was there.

Looking back on this, I can laugh (remember he was three), but my husband and I were not laughing then. We were caught up in the popular tidal wave of early childhood achievements and were scared of being left behind. We were not really interested in what was happening inside our son, only how he compared on the outside to other children. My angst was growing at what I perceived was his lack of forward momentum, so I looked elsewhere to provide this. When I went back to work after maternity leave, we paid a kindergarten teacher to come to the house three days a week and tutor our son.

Again, there was no critical point that I remember saying, "This is ridiculous. I'm not going to pay to send my child to school and pay a tutor and nanny at the same time!" Gradually, I realized that my son could stay home and play for free and in the meantime, maybe I could teach him something.

Around this time, my husband accepted a new job and we moved, so our family was primed for change. I started to work part-time and we realized we really couldn't afford private school on our new restricted earnings. I went to my husband one night and remarked to him that I felt I could teach colors and shapes just as well as a school, and kindergarten wasn't mandatory anyway – why not try teaching at home for a year? He agreed with me, and so we began our homeschooling journey.

I juggled my schedule so I could work nights, weekends, and holidays. I picked up a few books at our local bookstore and started investigating topics that I could teach my kids. When my son showed an interest in space, we went to the Kennedy Space Center, checked out every book and video on space and astronomy from the library, and went the National Air and Space Museum in Washington D.C. When Scotty Carpenter, a Mercury astronaut, came to lecture at a local university, we went to see him. I was subconsciously trying to do the opposite of what I had objected to in my son's preschool. Instead of a small school room and play yard, he was able to move through a variety of environments and instead of only playing with a few age matched peers, he was able to interact with people of all ages. He seemed to flourish with this type of living, even though at that time I did not consider it "education".

When the next year arrived, I went to our local elementary school and picked up a copy of the state standards for kindergarten and first grade. I was shocked to see that my son already knew everything on those lists and a whole lot more. I approached my husband with these facts and we started to consider permanently learning at home. The more we learned about homeschooling, the happier we became; we realized that we'd been homeschooling for the past year without knowing it. I still had a lot of trepidation and a big learning curve to go through, but we never looked back.

> ▲ Not every moment is fun and games though. My family likes to refer to a rather infamous example from my son. He had been learning about Neanderthals and early man at a natural history museum. He was enamored with the subject, and we continued studying the topic over the next weeks for our science lessons. That following weekend we hosted a party with some individuals from my husband's work wherein my son, then five years old, approached a certain gentleman and informed him that his skull looked like that of a Cro-Magnon. The poor man was stunned; what do you say to a kid that thinks you look like a caveman?

Reasons to Start Homeschooling

If you talk to any group of homeschoolers, you will get a dozen different stories about what spurred them to homeschool. Parents' reasons for homeschooling their kids are as varied as parents themselves. Some knew homeschooling was for them from conception, while others fell into it along the way. There are those families with constraints such as illness, travel, or lifestyle that make traditional schooling difficult. There are families with children who have special needs or are especially gifted. There are those children who excel at sports or performing arts who aren't able to pursue their interests within a traditional schooling framework. There are families who disagree with traditional school curriculums for academic or religious reasons. There are also those people who can't articulate a definable reason to homeschool; they just know it feels right for them and their family.

Many people that I meet start investigating homeschooling because of issues their children have in school. Consider the child who has already mastered a subject and is required to sit through endless repetition until the majority of the students have mastered the skill. Or the opposite scenario, when a child needs more work on a subject to master it but is being pushed along because the majority of the other students have already mastered the material. Schools must adopt a one-size-fits-all mentality for the schoolroom, but the children they teach aren't all the same. It doesn't make sense that a teacher is going to be able to teach a subject to twenty different children all of varying abilities, backgrounds, and personalities at the same time with the same method.

Many parents that I have known start to realize these problems with the school system as their children navigate their way through it, leading them to consider homeschooling as an option. Often they start this process while their children are still in school and they spend a lot of time agonizing over this decision. If this scenario applies to you, you can relax. The decision to homeschool is one of the few decisions in life that is reversible. There's nothing that ties people to homeschooling except the positive results it tends to have. You can always decide to change tactics if it's not fulfilling the needs of your family.

 HOMESCHOOLING HIGHLIGHT

Relax! Nothing is irreversible. Give yourself a chance to explore homeschooling without pressure. If you don't like what you find (although that's hard for me to imagine) you can easily resume your former traditional school model.

Actually Getting Started

Transitioning to a homeschooling lifestyle should be an enjoyable process for you and your family. If your child is currently in school, consider that you're separated from your child for a significant period of time every day. Even though the school day might only be seven hours long, with travel time, homework time, and extracurricular activities at school, there is a lot of time that you are not in direct communication with your child. As you look into homeschooling, it might be helpful to whittle down that time apart. Having your child with you as you start the process of looking into homeschooling is valuable for them because they get to be involved in a process that will affect them, but it also gives you a chance to begin reconnecting with them.

If there is a problem in school and you have thought about homeschooling, you might want to consider pulling your child out of school as you start this process. Many school districts will try to discourage you from doing this, but you do have rights as a parent. School officials will not want to let you do this because they often get funding based on attendance; however, you need to consider your child's needs over those of the school system.

Once you've decided to look into homeschooling, the internet is a great place to start. Just type in "homeschooling" and your state name into a search engine and you should get a few hits on the state homeschooling groups, which can then lead you to local groups. Don't be afraid to email people and ask about local gatherings and park days. Make sure you involve your kids in this process. Talk to them about the processes you are going through to investigate this topic. When you attend homeschooling functions, make sure you talk and mingle, but do it with your child at your side. They will want to play and socialize with other kids, and that is fine, but if they are shy and want to hang out with you, that is okay too. They will learn from listening to you talk to the other parents. Involving your child from the beginning will help you make decisions that are more likely to be successful in the long run.

Watching you go through the process is a lesson in and of itself for a child. It will help them to see decision-making in the process of happening and make it more real to them. Do not be afraid to show your children that you do not have all the answers. This will not make you look weak or dumb as long as you research and try to find solutions. This will allow them the ability to tackle things in their own life without fear – and many people today are held down by nothing more than fear of failure and fear of the unknown. Show your child how to break out of that box by example.

I don't want to imply that the decision to homeschool or not should be solely the child's choice. A child is not capable of deciding whether to be homeschooled or what they need to be taught. Remember, children work by the principle of immediate gratification. The concepts of delayed gratification don't fully develop until mature abstract thinking evolves, usually sometime in the adolescent years or even into young adulthood. However, because they are the focus of the homeschooling, their insights and observations will be invaluable as you chart their future course. You, as the parent who will absorb the burden of the work and planning, will need to be the final decision-maker. Beginning to homeschool will be a much easier and much more instructive process for everyone if your child is aware and has their input considered all the way along.

If you feel compelled to do so, you can tell the school what you are looking into for your child. Sometimes school districts require written notice in advance for absences and a simple letter to the administration should be sufficient. Some of the more supportive and enlightened teachers can even be resources for you, but many times it is better to keep your reasons to yourself and simply notify the school that your child will be absent for a day or several days. I don't want to alarm you or imply that there is any need for secrecy or subterfuge. It's simply easier to investigate your options without pressure. Also, if you decide to return to the school system, they will be none the wiser.

Don't worry too much about missing schoolwork, regardless of what the school says. Chances are if there is a problem that is leading you to consider homeschooling, not much learning and a lot of misery is going on. Your child won't miss much! If you are still concerned about upcoming exams or missing reams of schoolwork, there are other creative ways to learn about homeschooling with your child at your side. Go to a local homeschooling group park day on a vacation day for your child, a teacher planning day, or over the summer. Or you might want to start at a homeschooling convention, which are normally held over long holiday weekends. There are many ways to meet and learn from other homeschooling families while accommodating your schedule and your child's school schedule. But remember, there is no *crucial* lesson or day that can't be missed. They can all be made up with a little help and patience.

Not all homeschooling stories have a happy ending, and there's a lot that can be learned from the challenges that others have faced. A good friend of mine started homeschooling her two children when she realized the local public schools were not meeting her children's needs. My family moved and I lost track of them for several months; when we got back in touch, I was disappointed to find out the girls were back in school with the mom complaining that she couldn't get her youngest to do any work, specifically writing assignments. She voiced sadness over losing the homeschooling lifestyle, but felt she did not have an option. Another acquaintance homeschooled her child until high school, telling me that she felt having a teen at home would be too difficult during the high school years. Her homeschooling style and methods were directed towards younger children and were not flexible and adaptable enough to grow with her child. She also did not feel that she had the appropriate parenting skills, or anywhere to go to find or learn them.

When problems like the ones described above pop up, don't immediately think that homeschooling is not for you or your family. Rethinking issues and dilemmas and knowing where to go for information and resources can often solve many troubles.

How to Stay on Track

One of the most important exercises to do at the beginning of your journey, whether it's your first time beginning or you're turning over a new leaf, is to write a mission statement. Articulating your thoughts and feelings is extremely useful. This mission statement should be about your visions and long-term goals as the primary educator of your children. It will help define the direction of your homeschooling journey.

When I was first introduced to this activity, I was unimpressed; my gut reaction was something along the lines of, "Don't all homeschoolers have the same mission? We all want to teach our kids at home." Nevertheless, I continued with the activity, and as I did I realized that creating a strong mission statement is more complicated than I'd supposed.

> ♠ A friend of mine went as far as typing up a list of skills she wanted her kids to be familiar with or master by the time they left home. It was eclectic and comprehensive, covering just about everything from understanding how to arrange financing on a home or car purchase to knowing the multiplication tables. She mentioned to me that just going through this exercise was helpful because it caused her to step back and see her children's education as a whole rather than just the next month or so.

It took me about two weeks to come up with my mission statement. I revised it over and over again, tweaking words and phrases until I felt it really resembled my vision for my family. When I first wrote it (in my second year of homeschooling), I was so embarrassed by it that I kept it hidden in the notebook where I stuff the kids' schoolwork. It sounded way too high-brow, but the more I read it, the more I realized that it was true to me and my family's values; there was nothing embarrassing about it. I still have that original mission statement tucked into a notebook that I use regularly for the kids' schoolwork. Mine has held up over numerous changes in my family life, and though it may need to be adjusted at some point in the future, you'll be surprised at how resilient your statement can be. Long term goals and visions are usually not changed by the detours of life. Here it is:

"My mission in life is to teach my children and others to be tolerant and selfless, respectful of the earth and all the creatures on it, within the context of modern civilization, as well as to enable my children to achieve happiness, wealth, wisdom, and success in life by performing to my full capabilities and providing a role model to others for discipline, sacrifice, and the pursuit of a life-long education."

As I was writing this, I was struck by several things in my mission statement that I had not previously thought about. I mentioned my children and *others*. I had never really considered the people outside my family, but I realized that I did enjoy teaching and guiding others. When an opportunity came up for me to be a leader of my daughter's Daisy Girl Scout troop, I leapt at it. Writing my mission statement had helped to make this decision for me – it was a perfect opportunity. Many years after writing this statement, I had the opportunity to teach at a community college and again, this was an easy decision for me, because I had already articulated my desires for just this sort of prospect. I was able to explore a new path in my life without a lot of fear or concern of whether it was right for me. I knew it had been a desire for a long time and one that was synchronized with my goals in homeschooling.

The statement also taught me a lot about my homeschooling style. I realized that unschooling was not for us. I was too focused on external measures of success and achievements to allow the children to chart their own course. It also demonstrated my belief that education is not just contained in a school classroom between the hours of 8:00 AM and 2:00 PM, but rather is a life-long process. This has shaped many of our family's experiences and the way we go about homeschooling our children.

Some mission statements will encompass educational goals alone, while some will be ambitious and far-reaching, but make sure that yours is true to you. This exercise should take a while; to do it right, you'll need to think long and hard, and you'll probably want to confer with the other members of your family. Your goals, desires, and needs, as well as those of your spouse and your children, should be your primary material; what will help your lives to be fulfilled? This long-term vision will sustain you when things are not going well, and they'll provide a base you can come back to if you need to change direction on your homeschooling journey. Looking beyond the short-term goal of meeting the educational needs of your child to your long-term goals, whatever they may be, will help you to accomplish what you want as a parent and a person.

STEPS TO WRITING YOUR MISSION STATEMENT

Get your thoughts on paper. Don't worry about whether they make any sense or are in any order. Just getting them down on paper is good enough.

1. Think about what made you consider homeschooling and the benefits you want your family to receive. This will give you valuable insight into what direction your goals lie in.
2. Consider your long-term goals for yourself and your family. If you do not have any, don't be surprised. Many of us are so busy with the day-to-day and short term goals that we've never sat down and really thought about the future. Consider what's important and meaningful to you today and what you think will be important to you later in life.
3. Think of your day-to-day life. What are priorities to you, things that you make sure happen no matter what? Have you covered these already or do you need to add to them? Think of your family members

---

and what their priorities are. Do these diverge from or coincide with your goals?

4. Now look at those goals and see if they can be grouped. Are there certain areas that jump out at you as being more important than others?

5. Talk over your goals and priorities with your family and friends. Sometimes they can point out things you might have missed.

6. Now take a stab at writing your mission statement. First, just list things out. Don't worry about condensing it yet.

7. Prioritize your list in order of importance. If the priorities are different for different family members, make separate lists and see where those differences occur.

Once you have your thoughts down in order of importance, start paring down to the essentials. This is often the hardest part for most people, so don't worry if you get frustrated. If you do, just put it away for a few days and then when your mind is clear, bring it out again. Now, rewrite until the final product conveys your message accurately and succinctly.

Refer to your mission statement when making weighty decisions. Refer to it even when things are going well so you can give yourself a pat on the back. There are a lot of things that can come up and knock us off our course, and the mission statement will be there like a compass, guiding us back. Just because you are a veteran homeschooler does not mean that you don't suffer from a crisis of confidence and ability every so often. Kids, situations, and even you will change with time. A mission statement will help you not lose your way and keep your focus on what is ultimately important.

There are a million motivations for homeschooling, but they're all linked by the courage and determination of a parent or set of parents to improve their child's lifestyle and education. Once this momentous decision is made, it's vital to have a framework to rely on for support. Without that support, many problems and issues that are normally encountered along any journey will prove to be too difficult to overcome. This is the main function of the mission statement, defining your goals and helping you stay true to them. There are many other components to the homeschooling journey, but a solid foundation will allow the expedition to get off on a good footing.

3

The Socialization Question

The question homeschoolers get asked more than any other is, "What about socialization?" Many of us that homeschool feel the same way about this question as pregnant women feel when strangers try to rub their bellies. It feels like an invasion of our space and privacy. When you get asked this question often enough, there's an insidious process of worry and self-doubt that begins as you start to fret about whether your children are in some way "antisocial." It brings under scrutiny both our sanity and our belief system, indirectly challenging our assumption that homeschooling is a positive lifestyle decision. Understanding the motivation behind the question helps clarify not only why people ask it, but how it can be answered. The same way that belly rubbers want to feel the excitement of new life, people who ask the socialization question want to know that we aren't messing up our children or isolating them from the rest of society. In answering this one question properly and persuasively, homeschoolers can do more to further the cause of homeschooling than by doing just about anything else.

This question showcases the uncertainty that develops when people see others going against norms – and let's face it, traditional brick and mortar schooling has been the norm for a very long time. This question also highlights the many different definitions that people have of socialization and the varied ideas of how to achieve success for those different definitions.

Socialization means different things to different people. A traditional definition would be one that you can find in a dictionary, so once again, I pulled out my handy *Merriam-Webster Dictionary*, which gave me the following definition of socialization: "A continuing process whereby an individual acquires a personal identity and learns the norms, values, behaviors, and social skills appropriate to his or her social position."

This definition really struck me because I realized when I started writing this chapter that I wasn't even thinking about what "socialization" really meant; I was just thinking about how to convince others that homeschooled kids get to play with other kids and be "normal." As I really started to think about the whole concept of socialization, I became curious as to how many different components there are to it. These parts include your personal identity, learning about your culture, society, and your role in it, along with social interactions. These are important distinctions to make when discussing socialization, as whichever component the questioner is meaning will have to be addressed in order to make a meaningful response to their question.

In helping you get answers to the socialization question for others and for yourself, let's examine the different parts of socialization one by one, learn the components of each, and learn where homeschooling can trump the socialization that arises from traditional education techniques. Then armed with this knowledge, we will address specific concerns often brought up to homeschoolers and give you strategies to combat them.

Social Interaction

The lion's share of questions that homeschoolers receive on socialization have their roots in the social interaction side of the equation. After all, it makes sense that in order to become a functional adult fully integrated into society that you would have to have had practice getting along with and dealing with other people. How can a child learn this if they are shut up in their home without a chance to interact with other children? And while social interactions with age-matched peers are one component of social interaction, we must not forget about the importance of learning social interaction skills with people of all ages and abilities.

Peer groups are an integral part of learning the mores of social interaction. They are outlets where children can test out their feelings and actions without the constraints that are present in families, jobs, or other formal organizations. Peer groups can also provide understanding of feelings and developments in a child's life that it is hard for adults to comprehend. This can be especially true in adolescence, when parental memory of those tumultuous years fades and teen angst begins to show.

The problem that exists in traditional schools is that this part of socialization tends to trump the other parts of the equation, skewing the socialization process towards peer groups. Schools tend to segregate children from adults and children of other ages, so that many opportunities for wider socialization and learning are lost. Add on the fact that children in traditional school settings are so busy after school with homework, jobs, and extracurricular activities that they don't have much time for exploring social interactions on their own. The actual peer group interaction time of traditionally schooled kids is far less than many assume.

Given the fact that socialization has so many aspects, it's important to recognize that communication with peers is vital; however, it should not become the primary method of socialization for children. Exposure to a more varied and diverse group of people than age-matched peers can help children learn the skills of social interaction more effectively and completely.

Also, don't discount the importance of learning about social interactions within the family. Families are often less judgmental and more forgiving than peer groups while children experiment with coping strategies. A great example of this occurred just the other day as I was talking to a friend of mine about our children. One of her older children was very precise and responsible, organized almost to a fault. One of her younger children was more free-spirited and less responsible and organized. Her older child was resentful of the younger one, who he felt didn't pull his weight around the house with chores and such. Instead of just jumping in to solve the problem, this homeschooling mother decided to make it an important lesson on social interactions. She pointed out to her son that dealing with people that didn't perform up to his expectations is something that will follow him throughout life. He could someday be in a workplace and have a co-worker that didn't follow through on his or her duties or be a part of a group in college that had some members that didn't follow through on their assignments. As she pointed out to her son, resentment of the other person would become a hard burden to carry later on in life. Also, simply stepping in and picking up the work not done by the other person would not always be a feasible option. Given this situation at home, it was a great way to for her son to start developing coping strategies that will be able to take him through difficult situations in life.

Reflecting on this lesson that was being taught at home, it is easy to see how homeschooling leads children to better social interactions with all sorts of people in contrast to the lessons learned in schools. Schools cannot devote too much time on resolving interpersonal conflicts because it disrupt classroom dynamics. Also, given the ratio of adults to students, it is not always prudent to allow children to work issues out with others on their own.

As I was researching this idea of the place of social interactions in classrooms, I stumbled across a study concerning socialization from a teacher's point of view. One conclusion of the study was,"Teachers can take direct actions minimizing classroom conflict by socializing students into a classroom environment conducive to learning."[3]

This attitude is the reason people ask homeschoolers about socialization. For most people, socialization has nothing to do with turning out productive members of society or superiorly educated children. They are only wondering how homeschooled children learn to sit quietly and do as they are told, finish busywork in the prescribed time limit, get permission for bathroom breaks, and accept the norms of their environment. This question is rooted in the belief that a classroom environment is the culture and identity that children need to become acclimated to because that is the only way they can ever achieve academic success.

And in a typical classroom and a typical school, that belief is probably true. Children have to earn the rules for the academic game before they can "win." The key point for questioners and questioned alike is that homeschoolers are playing a different game, one that works with life after school as much as (or more than) last week's test scores.

Achieving success in a classroom means following the rules the school system has established. Unfortunately, most school systems have rules that aren't focused solely on what's best for children's academic success or their matriculation into society as functioning adults. Though I am sure these things are concerns, standards and rules are also based on union contracts, work rules, vacation, bus, and lunchroom logistics, state budgets, and working with school metrics like attendance and graduation rates.

To some extent, homeschoolers are a microcosm of what large school systems do. We also have to operate within budgets and schedules, but our constraints are those of real life, ones that children need to learn how to deal with to be successful and fulfilled. We also have much more flexibility in meeting the needs of our children because we can provide for them individually.

All of the these things I have talked about with social interaction are important components of this part of socialization. It certainly encompasses peer groups, but does not stop there. Being a functional adult in society means understanding social interactions with a wide variety of people and situations, not just those artificially created by the traditional school system.

Personal Identity

Another component of socialization is developing personal identity. As I said above, the main problem with socialization taught solely in traditional school settings is that it tends to be skewed toward peer groups and the social interactions that occur within these groups. The largest problem with peer groups is that they are by definition based upon conformity and sameness within the group, interested in collective qualities rather than individual qualities. While this can be a positive in learning how to negotiate complex social interactions, it can be a detriment while learning about your own personal identity. Learning about a personal identity within the confines of a peer group will develop an identity that is narrow, devoid of diversity and tolerance.

Self-creation, an important component of individuality, is hard to do when you're worried about conforming to an outside group with social pressures placed upon you. And in fact, the process of self-creation is just what schools aren't interested in teaching, as public schools are not interested in personal identity but rather collective norms that can be tested and measured. Teaching personal identity is too broad a focus for schools. The behaviors that are emphasized in schools are ones that are appropriate for the classroom situation, not the wider world as a whole.

The process of developing self-identity begins with social interactions even as a baby. When a baby coos and gurgles, parental response to those noises encourage them to make more. Children are taught from an early age that their actions can elicit good or bad responses in others. Learning these responses in the safety of their immediate family allows them to internalize and start to build their own personal sense of importance and guidelines of behavior. The premise of the school system we have in America today is that this foundation of self and family identity is being laid by the parents at home before school entrance at the age of kindergarten. This process is a continuum but by no means complete when a child reaches standard school age.

When you then take a child and put them in an environment where they are receiving reinforcement from others they aren't familiar with, you can have divergent ideas competing inside the child. Not all of these are disruptive, but it's easy to understand how this could inhibit the development of a strong sense of personal identity, if that personal identity is questioned before it is fully developed.

This process of developing a personal identity is widely divergent among families and children. It is dependent on many variables, which makes it impossible to say that each child has a solid grounding in their family unit and cultural heritage when they begin school. This is one of the wonderful things about homeschooling; with the constant access to the family it is a very natural and easy process to accomplish this goal in the way that's best for the individual child.

Learning about themselves and their family before other concerns intrude on their life allows children to develop a strong base and a solid personal identity with which to understand the world around them. They are ultimately more trusting and more comfortable with the unfamiliar. With a strong sense of self, children and adults can accept diversity in their surroundings because they're not afraid of losing themselves or what is meaningful to them. A strong self-concept has long been considered by many sociologists as the most important component in socialization, leading to improved abilities to adapt and integrate into society.

I have developed a simple pyramid I call the Socialization Pyramid. Akin to Maslow's hierarchy of needs, there needs a strong base constructed before anything else can be built upon it. Of course, acquiring a personal identity is a life-long process and one that will continually be re-shaped as your children age and mature; however, the building blocks are put in place in childhood. Very early on children need to be endowed with self-confidence and self-esteem.

It does seem difficult to accept on the surface, that eschewing the input of the traditional school system and concentrating on teaching from within the family unit will eventually lead to greater tolerance and acceptance and even a desire to learn about and embrace cultural diversity.

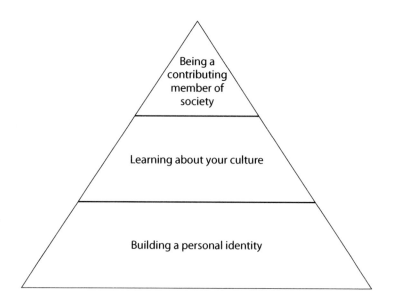

The Socialization Pyramid

But for many, the process of learning about one's culture and living in it is mainly handed down through the family or community. Not a lot of your own culture can be learned from others that are the same age, because they're learning as well. It's a part of your personal history, which can't be obtained from outsiders. How can one teacher in a classroom of twenty to thirty children be teaching them their own individual culture and cultural heritage? How can other children, age-matched peers, be teaching a child about their individual culture?

But again, living within your culture will require social interactions. It is important to have a range of social interactions across all ages and abilities. Maybe this is why the schools are turning out children that are so ill-prepared to deal with the issues facing them in adult life – what they have been taught bears very little resemblance to the way the world really is. Children in school are forced to conform in peer groups during the school day and while there are limited opportunities to obtain the other components of socialization after school and on the weekends, homeschooling provides a more complete frame upon which the full range of socialization rests. Both personal identity and social interaction can be woven into the very fabric of life without any extra effort or attention. Homeschooling allows children to find their place in the family unit, learn about their own unique cultural heritage, and address their adult roles in more public spheres.

♠ It is impossible to overestimate the importance of teaching children about their own identity and the sense of confidence that comes along with that. The confidence and esteem that arises from knowing who you are and knowing what you need and how to meet those needs is a valuable life lesson; without it a person can suffer from anxiety.

In private practice, when I was taking care of patients dealing with true separation anxiety – whether the parents were dropping off their children at daycare, school, or other activities – it could almost universally be boiled down to fear. The children feared the separation from the parents because they felt unable to meet their own needs; if a parent stayed behind, even if he or she was sitting in a corner of the room and not interacting with the children, there were very few problems and the children often went about their business even ignoring the parent. But when something happened that the child couldn't handle on his or her own, they would go from not noticing the parent to frantically searching them out. These children hadn't yet developed the mechanisms for understanding and coping with situations. Instead, they were relying on their parents to help them.

The traditional approach to separation anxiety recommended to parents is to trick children into getting absorbed into an activity so that they wouldn't think about the parental presence and then sneak out without the child noticing. This is counter-productive because children will notice eventually that their parents are absent, and that knowledge causes the child to become increasingly hysterical and clingy when separation is required in the future. The separation was not the issue, it was the lack of self-regulation inside the child. After teaching the child some coping mechanisms the problems would often fade away. Children that mastered self-regulation and the use of coping mechanisms were able to separate easily from the parent and be more flexible and adaptable to new situations because they understood they will not be at personal jeopardy; their internal situation has not changed, only their outward environment.

What Are The Arguments Against Homeschooling?

Let's start picking apart the cases against homeschooling one by one. By doing this I will dispel some of the common myths and misconceptions about homeschooling. I want you to feel confident that you are socializing your children in the best possible way, far exceeding what a classroom could ever offer.

How are homeschooled children taught to understand authority, hierarchy, and discipline without the controls that a typical classroom imposes?

As any homeschooling parent can tell you, we have a much tighter rein on the children that we teach when compared with teachers at public schools. When we are teaching our own children, we can look at them and judge whether they're paying attention or not and know whether they are being disrespectful or disobedient. Our learning time is not riddled with opportunities for our kids to hide behind others in the back of the classroom and pass notes, whisper, or text their friends. There is very little that gets by us, simply because we know our children better than teachers can.

In no way is our authority usurped by the rules and regulations of an organizing body that may or may not match our personal preferences. We actually have a better mode for authority and discipline because our children are not subjected to different brands or differing levels of enforcement by different people. We, as parents, have a code of conduct we expect in our family and that is reinforced in every aspect of our children's life, including their education. While parents who send children to school have to deal with some element of "deprogramming" when they come home, we do not. Our values, morals, and disciplinary system are constantly reinforced.

With children that are homeschooled, the consistency with which they are reared flows through all aspects of their life, including home, education, and extracurricular activities. They don't constantly have to assess and readjust their reactions and behavior, which leaves them more time and energy to devote to their learning and other activities. The consistency of the authority figures in their life allows them to feel comfortable and receptive, rather than defensive and dismissive.

How can homeschooled children ever learn to function in a group without learning in a group environment?

It's true that homeschooled students do not have to fight with other students to get a good pair of scissors, the unbroken crayons, the working glue stick, or any other of the myriad supplies needed in a school day. They don't have to guard their space in the school cafeteria line or shove to get access to a pencil sharpener. They don't have to wait with a raised hand to get a question answered. Rather, they have instant access to the supplies they need, the food they want and the attention they crave. In this instance, people that do not agree with homeschooling are right. Homeschooled children do not usually have to subjugate any of their needs in the course of a day because of peers, availability of supplies, or bureaucracy.

But don't think just because children are homeschooled that they do not ever have to subjugate their needs. The fact that homeschooled children are not forced to run the gauntlet of group dynamics in certain aspects of their education doesn't mean they do not have ample opportunities to learn how to share and work as a member of a team. The team they are on is just composed of family members rather than of other children their same age. A certain amount of learning to be happy even when immediate gratification doesn't occur is important.

Children of large families will especially need to learn to subjugate some of their needs as their parents will have duties they need to attend to with their other children. Homeschooled children with parents that work or have other commitments will have to learn that their own needs do not always come first and they might have to wait to get a question answered or help on a project.

In the course of a typical day, homeschooled students have to deal with siblings and their needs that might interfere with learning time. There are errands that need to be run, repair men visiting, meals being prepared, and perhaps the business or volunteer work of one or both parents to be dealt with as well. They get to see their caregivers prioritizing real problems and issues and they learn how they fit into those priorities. Children are exposed to the type of sharing that makes successful families. They learn give and take with real-life consequences.

More importantly, the type of sharing that homeschoolers learn is not tied to their performance. Schools might try to tell you they promote sharing, but the child that doesn't master the concept of "sharing" to his or her own advantage will never come out on top. Grabbing supplies or the front of the line might mean more access to the teacher or more time to complete a project that will ultimately give the child a better outcome. Homeschooled children are free to devote their learning time to learning, not worrying about the distribution of supplies or wondering whether their question will ever be answered. Even if they have to deal with other siblings in a large family, it is easy for homeschoolers to understand that the delay in getting their needs met is a real-life consequence that is an important lesson for life and not one artificially created in a traditional classroom environment.

When do homeschooling children get a chance to interact with other kids their same age?

Contrary to popular belief, homeschoolers don't (generally) stay locked inside their houses, shunning contact with the outside world. Homeschoolers have vast networks of play groups, park days, and other outlets for their children to experience playing with and interacting with other children.

The best thing about these opportunities is that they aren't only with age-matched peers or people that share the same first letter of the last name. Homeschooled students are forced to play and get along with children of all ages and ability levels. This helps develop tolerance, patience, and acceptance versus the intolerance and prejudices that the divisions of school-aged children promote.

Homeschooled children operate in a circle of people much wider than that of traditionally schooled children. Children in traditional school can very easily shun or be shunned by others that are older or younger both in their academic life and after-school activities, which are usually segregated much like a classroom. Homeschoolers bypass this segregation and are more open to associating with others that are older and younger. When left to their own devices, homeschoolers tend to segregate along lines of similar interest, not gender or age.

This familiarity and comfort level with all ages and abilities of others gives homeschooled children a broader experience in their world which translates into a better sense of their place in the family and community. This will lead to a deeper, better rooted personal identity and overall improve their chances for socialization.

If you homeschool, when are your children ever forced to deal with things on their own without mom and dad's help?

The constant parental presence on homeschooled children's lives can often be misconstrued by others as smothering and detrimental to children developing into competent, capable adults. The opposite is actually true; often homeschooled children are better able to meet challenges on their own than children that were traditionally schooled.

While this might seem contradictory, the reasons for it are readily apparent if you understand the homeschooling lifestyle. The close association between a child and their caregiver allows for constant modeling and mentoring to take place on all levels.

♠ When my son started learning Algebra, I struggled a little to recall problem-solving techniques that I had learned at his age. In order to be better prepared to answer his questions, I often hid the answer key and worked out the problems along side of him. When he missed a problem or had a question, I pulled my paper over and showed him how I'd solved the problem. When we ran across a problem that neither one of us knew how to solve, he could see me work at it and observe my approaches. In this way I helped my son with his subject work and exposed him to valuable problem-solving tools at the same time.

Constant parental presence allows children to learn from the way their elders handle things. Of course, parents can and sometimes do too much for their children, but that is not unique to homeschooling. It can happen in any family, and in my private practice I saw a lot more of it in the traditionally schooled children of working families where parental guilt about not being at home segues into an inappropriate need to do things *for* children and not *with* them.

The continuous exposure to parents gives homeschooled children more knowledge about how to act and live as adults than children without constant parental presence. They will learn about their culture and their place in the world much easier than children who have that presence only in certain areas of their life.

Aren't homeschooled children socially inept?

Sure, there are some homeschoolers that tip the scales on the weird factor, but there are far more children in traditional school that have significant social problems. Most homeschooled children are well-adjusted, articulate, and normal. Homeschooling by itself doesn't cause or cure social ineptitude.

There are many ways in which homeschooled students are perhaps better socialized than traditionally schooled students, but the biggest argument that can be made about socialization and schools today, is that they are obviously not doing a very good job. If it is important to socialize the way the school system recommends, then why are there so many children out there with poor personal identity and a lack of moral reasoning and judgment?

In 1994, Harvard University made an unprecedented step in character education. They were feeling rocked by the waves of scandals that were enveloping their former graduates in the form of insider trading, financial fraud, embezzlement, industrial espionage, and lack of accountability. Because of these highly publicized cases, the administration realized that some of their students were leaving the university with definite anti-social tendencies. This was a stunning revelation to the administration, because they had assumed this type of education was unnecessary, thinking by the time these young adults reached their classrooms they would already have a moral code in place.

The students that were entering Harvard were for the most part from traditional schooling backgrounds. They were well socialized in the educational definition of socialization but this definition did not encompass what happens beyond the classroom in the real world. Understanding this difference caused Harvard to institute a program of moral responsibility and reasoning. They added courses in moral reasoning and ethics as part of the subjects now mandatory for graduation. While this is a good start to try and correct this problem, the challenge for Harvard is trying to undo years of reinforced social norms that were formed by the student's peers and the school system.

Many of the problems that the administration of Harvard (and probably many other universities and colleges) deal with are ethics and values, which are closely tied to socialization. When children learn about their individual cultural heritage and their place in a family unit, they will gain a measure of responsibility and accountability that will allow them to develop values and systems of moral judgment that will prevent these problems from developing as children mature toward adulthood. A true and deep understanding of self allows children ,and subsequently adults, to engage in more meaningful relationships with others. Homeschooling offers children the chance to do this without the outside influence of a peer group offering judgments and opinions.

How to Deal With the Socialization Question

When someone asks you about how your children are being socialized, how will you respond? How can you convince people in a few short minutes that not only does homeschooling effectively socialize children but can even do a better job than traditional school?

As I have shown, socialization is a far more complicated process than just figuring out when and how much your kids get a chance to play with other kids. This is a crucial component of course, but there are also the other components like developing personal identity, learning about other's cultures and beliefs, and then finally fitting into modern society with all of its many facets. This process is a complicated one that often takes a lifetime to develop and refine. It is impossible to do it justice in the few minutes you have to answer when asked the dreaded socialization question!

But relax. Usually people are just worried about the social interaction part of socialization, and once you figure that out, this becomes a fairly simple question to answer. So start off by answering their question with a question of your own; "What exactly do you mean by socialization?"

If the answer to your question is the usual and expected one of asking when your kids play with other kids, often times simply cataloguing all of the various ways that your children experience others and have those opportunities for social interaction is enough to satisfy the curiosity of the askers. Pointing out that your children have opportunities for social interactions in a variety of settings even beyond what children in traditional schools experience can in and of itself be a powerful statement.

If, however, the questioner is actually concerned with some of the other aspects of socialization we have discussed in this chapter, feel free to launch into a more in depth discussion. If someone has an understanding of the process and components of socialization, it will be easy to showcase homeschooling in a positive light as it truly does allow for a more complete and individualized approach to turning out a fully socialized and contributing member of society.

So by simply turning the question around and getting at the basis of their concerns you will be able to figure out the right way to respond the socialization question and at the same time showcase the positive aspects of homeschooling. It's a valid question; have a valid answer.

4

Homeschooling Personality Disorder

In my second year of medical school, I took a particularly scintillating psychiatry course on mental disorders and personality disorders. We, the students, were confident that we would treat and serve these unfortunate people but the professor surprised us when he said that every student in the room could probably be diagnosed with obsessive-compulsive personality disorder. We tittered nervously as we considered the truth of this remark – it takes a certain degree of obsession to get into medical school, and we all knew we had it. We were classic examples of a diagnosable condition that turns out to be more common, and more positive, than we'd thought.

In the time I've been a homeschooler, I've noticed a sort of "homeschooling personality disorder" that develops and becomes more pronounced the longer an individual homeschools. It's not as bad as it sounds. Sure, there are some unflattering things we as homeschoolers do. Sometimes we make snap decisions based on stereotypes; we segregate; we pressure people to be like this, not like that; and we can be elitist with the best. (Worst?) But, we can also support each other through hard times; we tend to lead full, busy lives; we're active in our communities; and we use our creative, flexible, and adaptive sides in our everyday lives. Homeschooling Personality Disorder isn't good or bad, it just is what it is and needs to be recognized as such.

Here's a list of traits I've noticed accumulating around homeschoolers, or, if you prefer, symptoms of the homeschooling personality disorder. Like med students with OCD, some of these are positive and others... less so.

1. Tardiness

Parents of traditionally schooled children are usually very punctual, with much of their time centered around school schedules enforced by third parties that impose penalties for tardiness. Once you begin homeschooling, punctuality tends to slip a rung or two on the ladder of priorities, since there are fewer scheduled places to be and fewer people or organizations that care about exact times. After homeschooling for a few years, it seems like there's very little that needs to be done at a specific time. Homeschoolers often drift in and out of activities when they fit best with whatever else is going on in their lives. Just because a park play day "starts" at one o'clock doesn't mean everybody or even anybody makes an effort to be there at one o'clock.

This can be a very irritating habit if you are trying to schedule an activity that requires promptness. And in fact, there is a well-described phenomenon called the "homeschool flake-rate" that we as homeschoolers know about. Homeschoolers that plan activities needing promptness and assurance of attendance have learned that it is wise to extract payment up front and threaten to make sure others show up on time. The flip side of this, however, is not as bad as it seems. While it's rude to "flake-out" and not show up when you have committed, there can be good reasons for it. If you are in the middle of a teachable moment then the flexibility of a lack of schedule can be wonderful. The feeling that you can choose whatever course of action is appropriate at the moment is very powerful. It allows for all those little curves that life throws at you to be accommodated in order to provide the best outcome for your children and their education.

2. Vulnerability

Homeschoolers are particularly vulnerable to crises because their routines aren't fixed by the weight of large organizations. When a crisis occurs in families that send their kids to school, the children and parents are able to keep some semblance of normal routine – even if the children are kept home for a time to deal with the problem, their actions are steadied by the knowledge that eventually, they'll be returning to their normal routine. Sometimes parents and children cling to routine as they would a life raft; it provides stability and predictability when everything else around them has none.

As well, when a routine is fixed by an outside organization, such as a school, it allows the family to give up control of that one area of their life. Abdicating authority to another source creates a sense of freedom because there's one less thing to worry about in an otherwise topsy-turvy life. I have known several homeschooling families that have been concerned because they have had to abandon lessons in the face of a crisis because of life's other obligations. This sets up one more set of worries that ultimately add themselves to the burden of the crisis that is already there.

This is only half of the picture though. On the other hand, sometimes in the face of a crisis, continuing with a normal school routine can be stifling and counterproductive, causing feelings and emotions to be buried and subjugated instead of experienced and dealt with. The intimate exposure to adults as they work through these difficult times can be beneficial and will help children develop their own set of coping skills and the ability to deal with adversity in their lives. Many times the lessons that are learned from being involved and a part of the family every step of the way through difficult times are more important than the lessons that are being missed in the curriculum.

♠ In 2009, my mother developed a series of medical problems that culminated in a diagnosis of cancer. In the beginning, as events were unfolding, the kids and I dropped everything to spend time with my parents. At first, I was concerned about losing school work time. All of our lessons were abandoned for several weeks, while we focused on family.

As time went on though, I realized what important lessons the children were actually learning. We were learning about diseases, the medical system, and insurance. We also were learning about patient advocacy, dealing with medical professionals and institutions from a different side than I was used to. We learned about how a family can pull together in a crisis and how to handle stress.

When my mother stabilized and was back on her feet, we returned home and resumed our lessons. However, to this day, I feel the lessons the children learned will last them the rest of their lives. They will be stronger, more confident adults able to deal with problems hopefully more efficiently and with less angst.

If I had isolated the children from what the rest of the family was going through and tried to have them continue on with their "normal" routine, they would have felt left out and would have missed out on a lot of practical life lessons.

3. Insecurity

Homeschoolers can often be a touchy bunch. They're extremely aware of what they're doing and it's unusualness, something that is constantly reinforced in our society. In many cases, this hyper-awareness leads to the feeling that the homeschooler's efforts can never be enough. Believe it or not, I've seen this insecurity manifest itself in many ways, including through hysterical outbursts and panic attacks.

At the most unusual times we're blind-sided with thoughts along the lines of, "What are we doing? Are we ruining our kids forever?" This precipitates panic and hysteria as we wonder what we should be doing that we aren't already. Parents that send their children to traditional schools are immune from this, as they have abdicated any worries to the institution. So while at times this can be a huge detriment, it can also be helpful. If we can channel the worries and fears this insecurity brings on into careful review and attention to our children, we will always have superior outcomes for our children. After all, we focus on only our children, family and their needs while institutions will try to meet both the needs of the institution itself and all the children in it.

4. Generosity

Few communities are more giving in the sense of sharing time or resources with others. Homeschoolers don't need to have the competitive edge that kids in traditional schools do. We don't have to worry about being measured against others or against an artificial ranking system. Because of this, we are very willing to share curriculum, resources, and other information. Each individual success adds to our success as a community. I have seen homeschoolers spring into action at a moment's notice to help a new parent get answers to their questions or feel welcome at a gathering. When one parent discovers something that works, they are not stingy about sharing it; it gets immediately publicized by word of mouth or by an email loop.

♦ A recent post on a homeschooling loop I saw demonstrates this generosity. There had been a mom wondering about how to start teaching her son to read. She was soliciting recommendations from other homeschoolers on which resources they used and their thoughts on the subject. Within hours, there were dozens of posts with helpful suggestions and resources, along with offers of books, videos, and curricula to be donated to this mom for free. Some of these were very expensive items, and they were being offered with no strings attached other than they be returned after they were used.

5. Self-centeredness

"Self-centeredness" might seem like a strange list-mate for "generosity," but the homeschooling selfishness has nothing to do with hoarding resources. It refers to the homeschooling tendency to be so focused on ourselves, our needs, and our circumstances that we sometimes forget that what works for us won't necessarily work for everyone. We can pressure people to conform to our ideals of homeschooling when they aren't appropriate for that family. At gatherings of homeschoolers, newer parents are often bombarded with answers to their questions; some of these replies are supportive and constructive, but there are always at least a few replies that are denigrating to an individual's choices and needs or are even downright judgmental.

▲ Consider another recent example I ran across on my homeschooling email loop. A mom who had been unschooling her children for about two years was frustrated and fed up. She described her children as uncooperative and resistant to any academic work. She noted they had not learned anything in the past two years, and she was desperate to change their situation.

It was wonderful to see the slew of email replies that were supportive and encouraging, but there was one email in which a fellow homeschooling parent espoused the importance of modeling behavior as the only teaching tool necessary, essentially accusing the mother of not being a good role-model. The implication was that if she had been modeling reading, writing, and basic math skills effectively in her everyday life, her children would have been agreeable and cooperative and her unschooling experience would have been successful.

Sure, modeling behavior is important, but there is so much more to educating your children. We shouldn't judge others and their choices and needs, and we especially shouldn't base this judgment solely on what works for our own personal scenarios.

6. Tenacity

Homeschoolers aren't easily put off by failure. When they run into a brick wall, they either scale it or go around; with the number of options available, giving up is rarely necessary. When one method doesn't work, we happily move on to the next. Unlike teachers in a school system, we do not have to rely on the textbook already chosen for us or the agreed-upon methods and time periods for teaching a subject. We aren't too attached to notions of how things should be or how kids should learn, so it usually pays to keep working even on intimidating problems. To homeschoolers, failure of learning is more often equated to failure of the methods or curriculum versus the failure of the individual child. This is in direct contrast to the attitudes of traditional schools, where failure is usually regarded as a failure of the child.

7. Elitism

If there's only one homeschooling parent in a group, he or she will often be the center of attention, lying through their teeth about how "it's really easy," or "we love every minute of homeschooling." Even though we might try hard not to feel superior, when a parent says to us, "Oh, I could never homeschool my kids, it would be too difficult. How do you do it?", we do feel better. We puff ourselves up and say with a little smile, "Oh, it's not that hard!" And worse than that patent lie is the accompanying feeling that because we're still homeschooling despite its difficulties, we're better than whoever we happen to be speaking with.

What we fail to realize is that many homeschoolers couldn't get their families up, dressed, and out of the house with lunches made and off to school at seven in the morning if our lives depended upon it. Many of us survive on the fact that we do not have to go anywhere in the morning if we don't want to. We also can stay in our pajamas all day if we choose. We can ignore people we don't want to talk to on the phone because it's "school time." We can enlist our kids' help in just about any task around the house and call it practical-life application. And we can schedule a "teacher-planning day" – code for a day off – any time we please.

The benefits of homeschooling are great and the lifestyle is wonderful, but we also need to understand that not everybody wants that lifestyle. The reasons to not homeschool can be as varied as the reasons for homeschooling in the first place. In these cases, the parents have probably chosen not to homeschool with the same care that we have chosen to homeschool. This population, though, must not be confused with the vast majority of parents that have their children in traditional school because they have never given it much thought and it is the default setting for education.

8. Non-conformity

By definition, homeschoolers are non-conformists. We are choosing to educate our children in a non-traditional way. We become comfortable quickly with this non-conformity. It might start out in the realm of education, but it quickly spills out into other aspects of our life.

Homeschoolers are very good at looking at other established norms and challenging them. We are less beholden to society's expectations and are more comfortable with being the non-conformist in a given group. I saw this in myself even when I would take my children to a dentist or doctor or getting recommendations on home or car repairs. I was less willing to just accept recommendations without a full accounting of the reasons behind them. After becoming more comfortable with questioning prescribed norms, you will find yourself questioning everything in your life. You will realize that you can craft your life to your own specifications and have less worry about the expectations of others.

9. Reliance

Partially as a reaction to homeschoolers' insecurity, many homeschoolers form strong support networks. Homeschoolers have gotten very good at connecting with each other and offering support and help. Many homeschoolers have started very successful support groups and networks for just these purposes that have brought help and shared knowledge into the homeschooling community.

It is not uncommon to have many spin-off groups start from a homeschooling group, such as book clubs, cooking classes, and play groups. Homeschoolers not only share lifestyle tips but support in other areas of life as well. Topics such as parenting, money management, home repairs, and more are all commonly seen and discussed in homeschooling circles. All of this support is key for homeschoolers because much of homeschooling is the lifestyle that surrounds it and not the education itself. Once the lifestyle is set, you will find that the education part will fall into place almost effortlessly.

10. Community Involvement

One of the greatest character traits of homeschoolers is their openness and willingness to experience the world around them. More often than not, it is homeschoolers that take advantage of community fairs, public movie nights, parades, museums, and other special events. The world is an open book to us, with everything weighed and evaluated with the educational benefit for our kids in mind. We throw ourselves into theatrical productions, concerts, art exhibits, and causes we believe in. Even homeschoolers that are introverted by nature will find themselves gladly getting out and joining in, forgoing their natural personality as their zeal for the educational benefits outweighs all other concerns.

Notwithstanding the above points, we are all just regular parents. Many people assume that the personality they see among homeschoolers is something innate. I often hear people who don't homeschool say they don't have the patience or perseverance that homeschooling demands, but I can think of many professions that demand a lot more patience than homeschooling.

HOMESCHOOLING HIGHLIGHT

Anyone can homeschool. Don't ever say you can't if you really want to homeschool. It will teach your kids that it's okay to walk away from something because you are afraid of failure.

Think about being a teacher, a day care provider, or a counselor. These professions require a lot more patience. Homeschooling is much easier, especially since it's your own children you are dealing with, whom you know better.

When parents begin homeschooling, they aren't any different from other sets of parents. Some are more patient or more organized than others, but together they represent the whole range of abilities present in any other group of adults. Learning to homeschool is a lot like learning to drive a bus – everything seems to take more effort than you think it should, and at first nothing seems quite comfortable. People accustomed to outsourcing their children's education understandably feel uncomfortable about the thought of being in the driver's seat and taking more control of what and how their children learn, but with time and practice, everyone can be comfortable at the wheel. As homeschooling becomes more comfortable, your personality will adapt to fit the lifestyle of homeschooling and will complement the whole picture.

PART 2:
Highlighting the How-to's

5

Me, a Teacher?

The first major consideration in setting up a homeschooling routine is getting rid of all preconceived notions of when, where, and how learning should occur. For people who are pulling their children out of traditional schooling, it's wise to allow for as much as a month of "detox" time for every year of traditional school. Children need time to lose negative feelings about learning as well as assumptions about what learning means for them. This time is best spent with minimal focus on schoolwork; instead, it should be focused on creating a positive home environment and strengthening family relationships. These goals are integral to an effective homeschooling experience, so this time is far from wasted.

Parents also need this detox time, because getting used to having children home for significantly larger portions of every day takes some work. Even more importantly, parents can use this time to learn about their children in ways that they may not have been able to before. By observing their children with a homeschooling future in mind, parents can learn important things about how their children learn and what they're interested in.

For families who have already been homeschooling for a while, it's often helpful to take a similar but smaller break. Children can mature and change so quickly that parents often find themselves teaching to their children as they used to be rather than as they are. It's crucial to get to know your kids by watching them and their behavior closely.

THINGS TO DO DURING DETOX TIME

Play Games: What kind of games does your child prefer? Do they like word games, imaginative games like charades, or action oriented games? Do they like frequent rewards while playing to keep their interest? Do they have to win? Do they feel upset if they are not playing well? This will give you information on how to structure individual lessons. It will guide you on how often you offer rewards for work that is done and the length of assignments or projects.

Talk: Use open-ended conversation starters like, "What's your favorite food and why?" or "If you were an animal, what kind would you be?" Encourage your child to talk and share their ideas with you. This will give you valuable insight into their thinking and reasoning and might even help guide your choices of subjects.

Kid's Choice: Offer a variety of things to do and examine their choices – you might offer one day that your child pick from two or three different activities such as shopping and cooking a meal, a gardening project, or a craft project. The choice alone will tell you something as well as watching them work through the steps of the project. Are they good at organizing, creative, or results oriented? This will help you understand how much freedom they can comfortably handle with their learning.

Self-Directed: Do nothing and wait to see how your children fill their time - Do your children gravitate toward physical activities or quiet time?

Do they easily get bored and need adult intervention, or will they actively eschew help and suggestions? Observing their natural tendencies will tell you a lot about your children and their needs in education.

Once parents know both what their children need and want to learn and how they learn best, choosing what, where, and how to teach will seem natural. We'll cover the different styles of homeschooling later, but there are some principles of homeschooling that are applicable to every style and curriculum and should be addressed first.

HOMESCHOOLING HIGHLIGHT

Detox time is not wasted or lazy time. Don't underestimate the importance of time just spent observing your children. Resist the urge to be "accountable" for your time when you are observing your children.

When to Teach

People seem to grasp pretty quickly that we can teach concepts one-on-one in far less time than a teacher can teach a classroom of twenty-five or thirty children. One thing that takes a little more time to get used to is the homeschooling schedule; I'm always surprised when people assume homeschoolers do all of their work during traditional school hours. If we only worried about learning from eight to three each day, we would lose uncountable learning opportunities! There's nothing wrong with the typical morning school schedule, but don't feel obligated to have this arrangement. The schedule for my household changes depending on work schedules for me and my husband as well as when my children learn best and even what we did the previous day. We can stay up late to explore a concept or teach a lesson because we don't have to get up to go to school in the morning. It's difficult to pass up a teachable moment, even when they don't occur at the easiest times.

Often times, the burden of teaching falls on one parent's shoulders. Unfortunately, in order to afford the homeschooling lifestyle, one parent will usually become the sole breadwinner for the family. I'll focus a little bit more on this scenario because it's pretty common, but if you're in a family situation where both parents share an equal burden of work and homeschooling, consider yourself lucky. The principles below can easily be modified.

> ♠ One of my homeschooling friends has a husband who works the night shift. There's no way she can have a normal school day when he's trying to sleep, so everyone is up and out of the house in the morning and formal learning takes place in the late afternoon and evening. Another friend has a part-time job with variable hours. She has to constantly shift her schoolwork schedule around her job, causing some days to be early morning learning times and others afternoon or evening hours.

However, some basic consideration of when you will do most of the teaching activities with your children should be hashed out. Consider your preferences and those of your children, the work schedules of parents, and activities that you already are committed to as you think about this subject.

> ♠ In my household, my husband typically is busy at work while I am home with the kids during the day. Other than what the kids or I tell him, he doesn't get a chance to be very involved in our teaching. When I was working nights and the children were at home with my husband, he would often get to help with the schooling and finish up any lessons or do other work with the kids. This was a wonderful opportunity for him to get involved.

As my work schedule changed when I began writing, he didn't need to help out in the evenings because I was around. I naturally took over once again as I was the primary homeschooling parent. This actually was a detriment to everyone as he felt left out and even more removed from our homeschooling. I had to make an extra effort to include him again in a different way to accommodate our change in lifestyle.

The Learning Environment

When my husband and I were in graduate school, we had very different ways of learning. He had to sit at a desk with his book at a precise angle and his highlighters, pencils, and note paper in their predetermined places while I had to be on my bed with my books and papers spread rather randomly around me. We eventually rearranged our furniture with the desk pushed against the bed so that we could study together. Children and families have many different learning environments, and though they aren't always the same, they can usually be made compatible.

▲ Last year, I was having difficulties with my son in the mornings when we sat down to do our schoolwork. Five minutes into the lesson he would complain that he was hungry or thirsty, and every time he got up to get something to eat or drink, we would lose the thread of our lesson. I was beginning to think it was an avoidance technique, and one day I asked my son about it. I discovered that he had no problem with his work; his body just needed a mid-morning snack. Now my morning regimen includes putting a small snack and some water on the school work table before we commence teaching for the day. There are far fewer interruptions, and he really does perform better.

Along those same lines, I heard a speaker at a homeschooling conference several years ago discuss how she taught mathematics to her son. It was not his strongest subject or one that he particularly enjoyed. For many years, she struggled with all different kinds of texts and approaches only to figure out that those were not the stumbling blocks; it was the environment she was teaching him in. She discovered this quite by accident. She was out one evening at a church function and came home much later than expected. She had left some math worksheets for her husband to do with her son, and was surprised to find them finished when she came home. Upon querying her husband he said that they were done with a minimum of fuss. She couldn't figure this out, wondering, was it her that led to so many problems with math? The next day when she again assigned some work to be done in math to her son, he asked her if he could wait until later. Sensing an avoidance and procrastination but not wanting to disrupt the good chi of the day before, she said sure and just waited. After dinner, her son picked up his worksheets, and disappeared into his room. When she checked on him, he was sitting on his bed, with only a small lamp shining on his pages and the rest of the room dark. This was in marked contrast to the usual way they did math, in the middle of the day, at the kitchen table.

In asking him, she learned that he had a hard time sitting still and concentrating on his work with all the hubbub and distractions during the day, but at night, at the end of the day, he was content to sit and work on them in a quiet non-distracting place. She pulled out all the old textbooks she had given up on and found that he was very capable of working with them and did quite well when given all the other necessary environmental factors. At the time I heard her speaking, her son was in college, majoring in engineering, no longer needing a quiet, dark room at the end of the day, now that he was confident in his own abilities.

Environmental preferences are as diverse as the combinations of senses. They can encompass pretty much everything, including temperature, levels of light, noise, stress, and work, whether the learner is well rested or bored. Meeting the needs of children's optimal learning environments can be difficult, especially when they contradict the teachers needs or, in multi-student households, those of other children, but it's generally worth it. Children as well as adults learn better when they are comfortable and able to concentrate on the target material.

The easiest way to find out about children's optimal environments is observation, perhaps during a detox period. This is a great time to experiment with schedules. At what times do they seem to be tired? When do they wake up? Do they like to have set meal times and snack times, or do they follow an internal clock when it comes to eating time? Do they like to have noise like the radio or television in the background while they play, or are they easily distracted by stimuli? How well do they adapt to surprises or spontaneous activities? Given the choice, would they rather be inside or outside? All of these character traits translate into your homeschooling schedule: Children that like highly organized play time with complex rules will probably like an organized and precise learning environment as well, and vice versa. Understanding these needs in yourself and your children will greatly aid you in almost every facet of homeschooling, from setting up a daily schedule to choosing curriculum.

Learning Styles

Just as people appreciate different learning environments, people have different ways of absorbing and processing information. Ironically, parents that have had their children in traditional school will probably have figured this out before they start homeschooling. Teachers are usually pretty clued in to types of learning styles that are disruptive to the traditional school system and will be quick to point them out to parents. Children who learn kinesthetically (who learn better when they are moving) don't mesh well in classrooms with twenty-five other students. In my pediatric practice, I met this type of child about once a week because their teachers and parents assumed they had ADHD and therefore needed medication.

In addition to kinesthetic learners, some children are visual, auditory, or tactile learners, and some have more than one dominant learning style depending on the subject. I highly recommend the book *Discover Your Child's Learning Style* by Mariaemma Willis, M.S., and Victoria Kindle Hodson, M.A. It will help you evaluate both your and your children's learning styles and environmental needs. This is a wonderful resource that has sample questionnaires that both you and your child can fill out and score. It will help define not only environmental needs, but learning styles as well.

> ♠ Fast food companies learned about various learning styles a long time ago and quickly applied the knowledge to teaching strategies for their employees. Not only are employees verbally instructed and given reading material on how to build a taco or a hamburger, there are also posters in the kitchen that show whatever's being built in steps with pictures and no words. The diversity of materials along with hands-on experience can catch the majority of the learning styles of most of the people they employ. Instead of customizing their employee education or sticking with one method and hiring only those that can learn that way, this multi-pronged training program gives them access to more employees and trains those employees more effectively.

When I was in medical school, there was a saying about learning new procedures: "See one, do one, teach one." This was the mantra of learning everything from spinal taps to drawing blood. At first this terrified me as this was not the way I learned best. I could not "see one" and then "do one. It took me a while to figure out my learning style which was to read about the procedure, write down the procedure, and then try it, was different from the more conventional learning style of other medical students. I could almost skip the see one step as I was a very poor visual learner. I had to process the information first before I could internalize it. This was in direct contrast to some of my cohorts, who could see something and then waltz away with a complete understanding of the procedure. I was long convinced this was a deficiency in my ability to learn until a professor pointed out to me one day that this philosphy of "see one, do one, teach one" wasn't the only way to learn.

> ♠ I met a mom once in my practice who related an amusing story about her morning routine. Her teenage son resisted all her instructions. She would wake him up and tell him to get dressed and come downstairs for

breakfast, only to find him fifteen minutes later still in his room, definitely not ready for the day and sometimes even playing a video game. The problem got worse and worse until finally, out of desperation, she made a poster with pictures of all the tasks he needed to do in the morning. She laughingly told me that it was a miracle. With the poster put up in his bedroom, the very first morning, he was dressed and ready without any problems. It didn't take long for everyone to realize that he was a visual learner and not an auditory learner. When he got a set of instructions by the auditory method, being unable to effectively process them, he would just ignore them.

If your child is a kinesthetic learner, don't force them to sit still in a chair. Take the chair away and replace it with a big bouncy ball they can sit on. If they are an auditory learner, make sure you read them the instructions aloud for any worksheets they do before they commence working on them. If they are visually motivated, try to have as many visual reinforcements of concepts as you can.

When considering your learning style, think of your child, but don't forget about yourself either. If you and your child are very similar in temperaments, great, but there are many parents who wonder how the creature sitting in front of them could have sprung from their loins. Never underestimate your importance in this process. Remember that you're a huge part of the homeschooling experience; the way you're teaching has to feel good to you.

Where to Teach

If you or your children want to recreate a traditional school room, feel free – but don't feel that you have to. Kitchen tables make wonderful desks, as do floors, while couches and beds are great places for reading and listening. Also consider locations outside the home; there's nothing quite like a lesson about bugs delivered on a park lawn, and nothing motivates children to finish their lessons more than telling them they can play as soon as their schoolwork is done. It's more fun to learn about art at an art museum, earth science outside with a pick and shovel, and oceanography at the beach. Libraries are great places to learn about just about anything, including books themselves, and mathematics lessons can take place anywhere you can use a tape measure or a bag of candy.

Who Teaches

Although accommodating many schedules will mean having classes at odd times, recruiting other parents as teachers for small group classes is a wonderful way to tap into teaching resources. Extended family, neighbors, and friends are great resources for teachers and subject experts, and even if organizing a recurring class is too much of a commitment, most people are happy to share their skills or talk about their interests in a one-time event. I'm blessed with a father who knows practically everything about computers; even though he can't teach my children weekly or even monthly given our geographic separation, we all enjoy the little workshops he gives when we're able to visit. Many children love getting to know and interact with unusual people, and by learning from enthusiastic experts, children can learn to cultivate their own interests and talents.

▴ One of my son's friends was a gifted artist and was very interested in learning more about art and careers in art. His parents were wary of spending a lot of money on an art class because they had invested in some of his past interests only to see them abandoned before long. They wanted him to have some smaller experiences before committing a large amount of time or money. They searched through their local resources and found a neighbor who was a retired artist and an art instructor at a university. She was very willing to talk with their son and even give him some lessons.

Many homeschoolers also join co-ops and other group learning opportunities to take advantage of others' knowledge. I started a science club in our homeschooling group because preparing and conducting experiments can be time consuming and difficult. With a club, several parents can share the responsibility of teaching and each experiment can be observed and conducted by several students.

How Do You Actually Teach?

Now that we have covered some of the universal aspects of teaching, we can delve into the specific methods of homeschooling. For our simple purposes, there are three styles of homeschooling: unschooling, unit studies, and school-at-home. Rather than thinking of each style as a distinct entity, consider them to be points on a spectrum. Some of these styles will resonate more with you than others. Few people commit themselves exclusively to one style or curricula because children don't learn everything the same way in every situation.

Each style of homeschooling has its pros and cons. These pros and cons will be somewhat dependent on the family as well, as some aspects of each style will mesh with certain families and not with others. So it is very hard to categorize the good and bad of each style as some of this will have to be determined individually as what works well for your child and family.

Unschooling

The term "unschooling" was popularized by John Holt, an educator and writer whose studies and observations led him to the conclusion that children need to be led by their interests and desires rather than having outside educational standards imposed upon them. Unschooling will be different in its specifics for every child because it means following the interests of the child as subject matter and concepts are introduced. Some parents might wait for children to express interest in a subject before teaching it, while others might introduce a variety of subjects to see what appeals to the children most. Some children might be more methodical than others and want more structure than others, but the fact that it is child-led instruction makes it unschooling.

Unschooling itself has drawn criticism from many fronts as people tend to equate unschooling with "unparenting." Really nothing could be farther from the truth; people that are concerned enough to research educational styles and teaching methods are involved parents. The benefits of unschooling are enormous to those children who function best with self-led learning. It allows them to expand their learning along the lines they are interested in and pursue interests that they would otherwise not have time for. For those children who are not self-motivated, this might not be the best style, but even then, if you can find the spark that ignites their interests, they will take off and surprise you with the tenacity with which they pursue knowledge.

School-at-home

School-at-home is categorized by a parent-led teaching style, which means that the parents pick the subject matter and order of introduction. There are some people that have set lesson times and definite goals for each day; others have no plans and simply accomplish what they can in the course of a day. Some purchase a pre-made curriculum that has everything planned, and others choose their own materials.

School-at-home can be comforting to children who thrive on routine and are motivated by pleasing others. This can also work well with families that have mixed schooling, meaning some children in traditional school and others that are being homeschooled. Make sure though to leave enough time for pursuing interests outside of the chosen curriculum.

Unit Studies

Unit studies mix elements of school-at-home with unschooling. In unit studies, students take a single subject (sometimes selected by the parent, sometimes by the child) and learn about it from every angle. This teaching style works from a single point, such as a child's love for the ocean, and branches into related topics, such as literature based around the sea, history centered on seafaring explorers, the science and mathematics of salinity, pressure, and buoyancy, geography through coasts and islands, and so on. Unit studies can also work well with children who have an intense dislike of a particular subject because that subject can be introduced through a way the child enjoys.

> ♠ I once had a patient in private practice who loved ballet and planned to become a famous ballerina. She was quite talented and had a real future in front of her; however, she hated history with a passion. Her mother was bemoaning this fact as her daughter was in danger of flunking history in high school when I suggested to her mom that she start with the history of dance and ballet. The mom called me several weeks later to tell me her daughter now had a B in History and that she even enjoyed it, now that she could relate it to her passion.

Unschooling, school-at-home, and unit studies are three very arbitrary divisions to the methodology of homeschooling that encompass most of the homeschooling styles. Things are not this simple, of course. Within each of these basic styles are many further divisions. There is the Charlotte Mason technique, radical unschooling, classical education, and lapbooking, just to name a few. Even within each technique there are subtle variations that will occur as the method is adapted to each individual situation. Each one has had reams written about it and I invite you to look for further resources on the style that best fits what you, your child, and your family needs. I have included a list of resources and a little more explanation of each in Appendix A.

What to Teach

You can't teach everything and you don't have to. Your mission statement will help you prioritize your time and allocate your resources correctly. Pick out what you want your children to know and what your children want to learn and don't worry about the rest. If kids have developed a lifetime love of learning, they'll be able to learn the rest on their own.

I'm not going to spend a lot of time with this topic because mountains of literature have already been published about it; grade by grade state standards for education are available on the internet, at the local school board office, or even at your local public school; many books have been written about grade by grade subject matter;[4] and most curriculums will include a list of suggested subjects and content by grade level. Aside from traditional educational sites, there are many homeschooling sites that list books and subjects by age or grade. For older children, I recommend getting the admission requirements from a local college. Students who aren't considering college can find similar requirements for whatever they plan to do after their graduation; either way, it's important to have an idea of what student and teacher are working toward, which will in turn make it easier to know what to teach.

⚑ Teaching to published standards alone can be dangerous, as exemplified by the Medical College Admissions Test. In days of old (defined by the year I took it in 1989 and before), it was a multiple choice test designed to measure an applicant's knowledge base, critical thinking ability, and problem solving skills, all of which needed to be exceptional to begin the study of medicine. One important thing it did not cover was writing ability. Medical schools were being confounded with the number of students who didn't possess the most rudimentary skills necessary for writing in the medical profession. It wasn't that their students were not smart or capable, it was just they had been focusing on the material covered by the test. English and composition classes were seen as unnecessary when the time could be better spent mastering organic chemistry or molecular biology.

After years of pressure, the MCAT test started to include a written essay portion that would be factored into the overall score. Now of course, students are scrambling to make sure they can write legibly and coherently for the sake of the test.

Also, consider that certain subjects traditionally taught in a certain age range might be better introduced earlier or later for your child. A lot of parents who are inculcated to comparisons with other kids will find this premise very hard to follow, especially when it is a child falling behind their peers rather than leaping ahead, but don't panic. There are many other subjects that you can concentrate on while you're waiting for a particular skill to develop. If you have to cut a large portion out of teaching because your child is not ready, like reading or writing, replace it with geography, music or art appreciation, a foreign language, or a sport. This will allow your school day to remain complete and give your child a chance to excel at another subject. Then when you come back to the previous subject, you will not feel bad about any extra time you spend on it because you're ahead in other areas.

▲ Another homeschooling mom I know jumped on the reading bandwagon when her child was five. All the public school kindergartens were teaching beginning reading skills, so she supposed that she should too. The ensuing battles between her daughter and herself put enormous strain on their family, which spoiled a lot of potentially good experiences for them. Finally, the mother decided that for the sake of her family she would table the reading issue for a time. Several years later, when the daughter turned nine, she finally became interested in reading, and they turned back to it. She caught up to her peers within six months and is now happily reading everything she can get her hands on.

Don't be afraid of rotating subjects as your child's interests or abilities change. You might not need to teach every subject every year. Most schools hold their students to six or seven core subjects at a time in the elementary years and by the time college years come, most students are taking only three to four subjects at any given time. The time savings of one-on-one teaching does allow a little more of our schedule to free up, but it's important to resist the temptation to teach too many subjects at once. Sometimes it can be helpful to start a master list of every subject you would like to teach and of all the ones your kids have expressed an interest in. Prioritize the list to get what you want to start with, and then as certain subjects drop off, add others. This way at least you will feel that you have an orderly approach and won't leave anything out.

The Importance of Being Flexible

The key word to choosing a homeschooling style and curriculum is flexibility. Do not think you will find the one method or one curriculum that will meet all of your needs throughout your homeschooling journey. As with any journey you undertake, be prepared for the unexpected. It is those unexpected moments that you will treasure and remember.

▲ Just recently I had an experience which showed how much flexibility is needed in the homeschooling lifestyle. Nobody felt like "school," so I decided to take the kids to a science center. I was thinking fun, educational, can't go wrong.

Things did go wrong. The kids had a lousy time, with the gist of their complaints being along the lines of "Mom, we've seen all this stuff before. These are baby exhibits!" I was aghast at the truth of their pronouncement. I was still back in their earlier days of wide-eyed wonder and amazement at the simplest of experiments. They'd moved ahead and I hadn't.

I was upset about this for a while, but then I realized that this was one of the magical moments that homeschooling provides. Think what would happen with the same situation in a traditional school. They would attend the science center field trip whether they wanted to go or not, regardless of what their knowledge level was; if the exhibits were things they were already familiar with, too bad, learn to stand around and be bored. I was getting immediate feedback from my kids and being offered a chance to make an immediate change to fit their needs. So we left. I was an instant hero in my kids' eyes, and I used it as a teachable moment to show them just how much they had learned under my tutelage. Then we went home and did a science experiment that they didn't find irritating or beneath them.

However, as a homeschooling parent, keeping up with your kids is not easy. As you, the homeschooling parent, go through this process with your children, you will hone your skills and knowledge. You will also have expectations and needs that will change as you go through the homeschooling journey with your child or children. Some will be obvious; the birth of a new child or a move will take more of your time, while others aren't as obvious. Emotional stress that can occur with a spouse, illness, or aging relatives will wax and wane with time. You might need more prescribed teaching materials at certain times than at others. I recommend that you ask yourself the following questions once a month about each one of your children. These can become especially useful to ask when your children reach the teenage years and seem to grow and mature rapidly.

1. Has their physical or emotional situation changed in the past month and if so what are their new needs pertaining to it?
2. Have they seemed to have taken off or fallen behind in any particular area of study or activity?
3. Can I anticipate anything happening in the coming months that I can change now to prepare for?
4. Have they mastered a subject and is it time to advance them or drop the subject and add a new one?

I also recommend asking yourself these questions once a month:

1. Has anything changed in my physical or emotional situation and what are my new needs?
2. Have I lost interest in teaching any particular area, or have I developed any new interests that I could add?

Don't be afraid to admit that you're tired of teaching something. There's only so much that a person can take of teaching math to a kid that uses every free moment to exclaim how much they hate math and how much torture do they have to endure at the hands of their evil homeschooling mother. It might be time to change, and instead of drilling on those multiplication tables, switch to data collection and graph making. You might find the break turns your child onto math again and when you return to multiplication, they are happier (or at least, less resistant).

Also, feel free to tailor your homeschooling experience to your tastes or interests. In our homeschooling group, a mom recently pointed out to everyone that it was National Poetry Week and recommended that everyone bring one of their favorite poems to read at that week's park day. I realized that I never studied poetry – being a pediatrician, my schooling was heavily weighted to math and science. So, when my family had a lag in our literature curriculum (defined as, nobody could agree on what to read next), I checked out a book of poetry from the library, researched poetry on the Internet, and started to study that for our literature.

The best thing about homeschooling is that you do not have to allow anyone to tell you what your child needs. Listen to your children, yourself, and your family.

6

Curricula & How To Use It:
The Choice Is Yours

I like to define curricula as any item used to teach a concept. Most of us think of textbooks and lesson plans when we say curriculum, but any learning aid or tool can also be included in the broad definition of curricula. There are many non-traditional curriculum items that are useful, such as museum learning guides, DVD's, computer programs, and even other people.

When I was teaching my daughter a mathematics lesson which involved learning the seven times tables, there was a lesson plan that came with my math curriculum containing textbook problems, a computer game on the automated part of the curriculum, and a workbook that had multiplication practice work pages. In addition, we had a hand-held math computer game, math manipulatives, and a press-and-reveal plastic multiplication square with all the times tables on it from one to nine. All of these expensive, space-occupying pieces of curriculum were left sitting safely on the bookshelf while we got down her dolls and their clothes. We selected ten dolls that were going on vacation (had to throw in some geography, didn't we?), then started with zero dolls and then kept adding one to the group. Each doll packed seven items of clothing, and each time we added another we would write down the corresponding multiplication fact. Amanda learned her seven times tables and had fun, and I realized all the other things I had were a waste of money, at least with regards to this lesson.

This happens all too frequently with homeschoolers. We get all excited when we see the bells and whistles attached to expensive learning aids and overlook the basic facts of whether they will be useful in teaching our children. Of course, not everything can be taught with everyday toys, but there are some pieces of curriculum that are more useful than others.

About once a month, someone in my homeschooling email loop will request information on a certain textbook or curriculum wanting to know others' experiences with it. While it's always helpful to gather information, other people's experiences are often inapplicable to your family's circumstances. It is helpful to hear what others have to say about certain curriculum materials, but always consider your child and their learning needs when you make decisions.

At first this whole process of acquiring curriculum stumped me. More often than not, everything that I got – no matter who suggested it – would get very little use.

⚓ Even when you think you've found a winner, unforeseen problems pop up. A good friend of mine bought a mathematics curriculum from an exhibit hall booth at her state homeschooling convention. Her daughters were drawn to this booth over and over, and the family stood for hours watching the demonstrations and use of manipulatives and games that went along with the set. The curriculum was very expensive, but with the enthusiastic endorsement of their children, they went ahead and purchased it. I called her several weeks later to find out how it was going. Unfortunately, she was miserable. They finally had given up on the curriculum because without the man they had met at the booth actually doing it in front of them, it was too complicated to use!

To some extent the choices will have been narrowed down for you at this point because you know your preferred style of teaching and your children's preferred style of learning. Even so, a lot of success depends on the style and mode in which materials are presented. There aren't many hard and fast rules. For example, a kinesthetic learner for whom you would never ordinarily consider workbook material might benefit from a small amount of appropriate workbook practice in a subject area of strength to help build confidence and bolster skills needed to attack subjects that are more difficult. There's no magic formula into which you can plug all your variables to get the name of the perfect textbook; there's no substitute for researching your options.

I will introduce various traditional and non-traditional curricula materials along with some basic considerations of each type. But remember, in the beginning a mix and match approach might be best while you determine which type works best for your child.

Curriculum-in-a-box

One of the most traditional styles of curricula available are those that completely lay out the learning for you, grade by grade, with lesson plans, textbooks, and regular assessments. I call these curriculum-in-a-box. Depending on the company, they will usually contain all of the supplemental materials needed. They cover core subjects and are usually complete, all-encompassing, and inflexible.

When looking for a curriculum-in-a-box, I would encourage you to make sure you have access to it first before purchasing. Often, a good place to experience these is at a homeschooling convention. Companies will set up sessions that will walk you through their curriculum allowing you to get a more in-depth look at them. I've known several homeschooling friends who purchased curriculum-in-a-box over the internet only to be extremely disappointed with the results because of peculiarities that were revealed only with hands-on work.

Curriculum-in-a-box doesn't always have to follow the traditional rigid school-at-home approach. Obviously, that homeschooling style works well with curriculum-in-a-box since lesson plans are laid out with schedules that can be easily incorporated into this homeschooling style. A curriculum-in-a-box set could also be used by an unschooler who waits to teach a subject until it is brought up, but once it is, needs a structured approach to it. Curriculum-in-a-box can be used with any homeschooling style.

Because an adjunct to curriculum-in-a-box, there are subjects-in-a-box. This is not a complete set of core subjects, but rather one subject laid out in the same way as described above with set lesson plans, assessments, and materials included. This can be helpful when you like the treatment a company gives one subject, but not others. This way you can mix and match different subjects from different sources to best fit your child's needs.

Many people new to homeschooling will gravitate to this format, as it seems comforting and thorough. It's basically a re-creation of public school in the home setting. Parental participation is minimal and there's little advance preparation. Some of these programs even go as far as giving parents a script for teaching the lesson.

When they are chosen after lengthy consideration, these curricula can be wonderful and useful. If they are chosen out of parental fear or lack of confidence, they will probably be of little use in your homeschooling endeavors.

♦ A family my husband worked with had a daughter who was on her way to being a top-ranked tennis player by the age of thirteen, when her coach sat down with her family and discussed how much commitment that ranking would take and how they would need to adjust their schedules. She needed to spend more time on the court and less in school and she needed to be able to travel and accommodate tennis tournaments into her schedule. She had been doing very well in school and the family had a very ordered schedule with several other children in school. A curriculum-in-a-box was exactly what this family needed. The family's long-term goals were met, lifestyle issues and the learning style of their daughter was considered. It was a perfect match and this family has continued homeschooling very successfully.

Remember that just because you buy a curriculum or subject-in-a-box doesn't mean that you have to follow it. There is nothing wrong with using the parts of it you like and ignoring the rest. This is usually in direct opposition to the claims you will read in the introduction of most any these programs, which warn you that without a careful following of their plan and a systematic approach (their systematic approach) you will be unsuccessful achieving the goals of their curriculum. While that might be true in some cases, it's generally just a scare tactic. Give yourself permission to tear it apart if needed to better suit your child's needs.

Many parents that are Type A also gravitate toward curriculum-in-a-box because it assuages their internal needs for accountability and structure. Don't feel bad if this describes you – it describes me accurately. Remember that homeschooling is a relationship between a child and parents and must consider the needs of both of them. If you feel that curriculum-in-a-box suits your needs but does not match those of your child, don't panic. There is a way to consider both of you. Figure out what you like best about the curriculum. Is it the checklists, tests, or schedules? Is it the careful scripting, or the teacher's manuals? Once you figure out what appeals to you, you can take those aspects into other curricula that better meet your children's needs. If you like schedules, but your child likes reading real-life books instead of textbooks then draw up a schedule for those books instead. The possibilities are endless and might require more work on the front end, but if your child learns better in the long run, it will be well worth it.

Textbooks and Workbooks

The next big category of curricula involves a textbook approach. These use traditional educational materials in textbooks and workbooks, but instead of them being chosen for you and integrated into a complete schedule, you get to put together the individual pieces of your curriculum. Using textbooks makes it easier to follow educational standards while still being flexible. You can choose different grade levels in different subjects, decide what parts of the texts to teach, and design your own schedule to introduce the material. This approach can be highly effective for children who have widely variable levels of mastery in different subjects or for children or parents who need some structure. Textbooks are available in teacher supply stores, bookstores, college bookstores, or through on-line outlets.

Workbooks are a good adjunct to textbooks. Workbooks are available any place you can find textbooks. There's a lot of variation in style, presentation, and content, so it's important to look at these before buying them as well. The same grade level workbook on grammar can either be writing intensive, oriented only toward test-taking skills, or basic, depending on the company that published it and the standards followed. Some workbooks are very visual and others are very repetitive, so make sure you know what you're buying.

Many parents have successfully taught subjects out of workbooks when their children needed more hands-on practice with a subject. Workbooks generally require less teaching and more active involvement on the child's part, but still provide a level of structure and accountability to homeschooling.

Textbooks can be very expensive if they're purchased new, but there are many avenues for obtaining used texts. The first is your local public school. When a school phases out and replaces textbooks, they are usually sent to a book depository; finding out where that is for your area can be a tremendous help. In one community where I used to live, the public school district book depository opened its doors once a quarter for anyone to come and take as much as they could carry – for free. Most of these books are in very good condition, with little or no writing in them.

Also, many times homeschooling groups or conventions will have a designated used curricula sale or swap event. Many textbooks and non-consumable workbooks can be found at these events. Often times, many local schools have book fairs for their students and parents, and they are more than willing to open their doors to homeschoolers. Even though many of these items can often be purchased directly from the publisher or another outlet on the web, make sure they allow returns. Like the curriculum-in-a-box, there aren't many substitutes for looking at and holding a text in your hands to evaluate it.

 HOMESCHOOLING HIGHLIGHT

Look before you leap! Getting to hold a textbook in your hands and being able to show it to your children can be instrumental in saving you money. Often what you think is cool won't match what your children think is cool.

A treasure trove of good textbooks can be found in college bookstores, especially those that are located off campus and specialize in used books. Many used books are in excellent condition (they were probably never cracked open) and available for a fraction of the cost of new books. While many texts will be too advanced, there are a surprising number that can be used to teach middle- and high-school aged students. Remember that many freshman college courses are nothing more than a review of material presented in high school classes because most colleges find the average high school student woefully unprepared for higher level academia. In addition, many colleges are starting to post course outlines, syllabuses, and lesson plans on the internet. Not only can these be used to guide your choice of subject material, they're great tools for measuring whether you are properly preparing your high schooler for college courses.

In the past several years, more and more textbooks and workbooks are being published that have been written by homeschoolers for homeschoolers. This has broadened our choices of curricula immensely, as these texts tend to be friendlier to our way of instruction. But just because a book was written by a homeschooler doesn't mean it will be great for you.

Non-traditional Curricula Items

The last type of curricula includes all the non-traditional items that you can think of, from non-fiction books to DVD's, often lumped into the category of enrichment items. These are a homeschooler's paradise. Original writings and classic literature are a wonderful source of learning. They remove the perilous abridgment that texts serve up and often give a more complete understanding of the time periods involved.

One source of educational materials rarely tapped can be found through corporate America. Most large companies have active public relation or education departments that can be successfully leveraged for learning materials. Technology companies, theme parks, zoos, and environmental organizations have tons of educational materials and resources available.[5] These are primarily advertised to teachers, but homeschoolers are usually happily accommodated. Of course, these materials are created primarily as propaganda for their organization, so a healthy dose of skepticism is required, but in a way that increases real-world learning potential.

In addition to corporations, government organizations usually have many educational resources available as well. Probably most well-known is NASA, but there are many others like USGS (United States Geologic Survey) and even the Department of Energy. Just about any government site has an area designated as a "kid space" or "for teachers". Your tax dollars pay for these things; you might as well use them.

Trade books

Trade books[6] are another great source of curriculum, both fiction and non-fiction. Biographies are a great way to learn about not only history, but science, math, the fine arts, and language arts. Learning about the social mores and political situations of the time make certain things all the more fascinating. For example, when learning about astronomy and the solar system, look for historical accounts of Copernicus and Galileo to help round out the learning. When learning about density and displacement, knowing about Archimedes and his naked run down the streets of Sicily shouting "Eureka" can make even the most hardened math-hating child smile.

There are benefits to using multimedia technology as well. The amount of information that humanity has amassed is huge and keeps growing. Children today not only need to know all the basic building blocks, but they also need familiarity with the modern knowledge that has been discovered. Both of these need to be learned in order for them to be able to some day contribute the next layer. There is a lot more that needs to be learned and the visual medium is a powerful tool in presenting this information.

♠ I was struck by this realization first-hand when I was reading about medical schools and the anatomy courses they typically hold for their first year students. These students learn anatomy, confront death for the first time, and spend hours upon hours hunched over a shriveled, smelly, preserved human body, arguing with a lab partner about whether that string of unidentifiable tissue is really part of the brachial plexus or not. I have vivid memories of going through this process - almost a rite of passage. This method of teaching anatomy has worked for hundreds of years, but recently some medical schools are challenging these entrenched practices. The argument is that they are running out of time in the four years of medical school to teach the necessary amount of information. There is so much more known about the human body now, and more being discovered every minute, that something just has to go. Several schools have moved to teaching with a combination of preserved, pre-dissected specimens and a concurrent multi-media presentation to teach human anatomy, with very good results. Early studies are showing there is no difference between the two methods of teaching.

Multimedia resources can be found in just about every situation. Most museums, nature centers, and landmarks will have a short video presentation available that delineates their collections, points of interest, or history. My family always makes sure to hit these as close to the beginning of our visit as possible to help give us a point of reference for later in the visit. And don't feel that you can only use approved "educational" videos, or that somehow the learning has less merit if it is a piece of popular media. When we were teaching my son about the history of the space program, the movie "Apollo 13" was at the top of our list. Sure, it was a Hollywood blockbuster, but it had a lot of historically accurate information in it. We visited Kennedy Space Center, watched HBO's series *From the Earth to the Moon*, and read Gene Krantz's book *Failure Is Not an Option*. Combined with reading the Jim Lovell book that it was based on (*Lost Moon: The Perilous Voyage of Apollo 13*), he now has a very complete view of the time period and the Apollo space program, better I think than any textbook could have presented.

When you begin to look outside the realm of 'traditional' school materials, you can see that just about anything can be used to teach. A psychologist friend of mine once told me that the more pegs you can hang a piece of knowledge on, the more likely you are to remember it, and the less likely it will slip off and get lost in the bottom of the coat closet of your mind. The strength of non-traditional curricula materials is that they present many pegs for the mind as opposed to the page or chapter a textbook provides.

When shopping for curricula materials, try to start small. It's worth trying out a few products before committing a lot of money into resources. Once you find something that works, don't go overboard and ignore everything else. Different subjects require different approaches. It's best to keep an open mind every time you approach buying curricula for a subject and start from the beginning each time. It will rapidly become apparent to you which curricula are successful in each subject and which aren't working. Often, even the youngest of children can give you feedback on items and express their opinions. When children start complaining and fussing about doing schoolwork and it becomes a drag to teach them, one place to look is the materials being used.

It's best to draw up a budget for what you can afford and then prioritize it with your goals. Don't spend $300 on the newest and greatest foreign language program if that's not at the top of your priority list.

And if there's an expensive piece of curriculum you feel you just have to have, look around and see if you can get it used first.

Just as there's no one method of homeschooling that's best for all, there's not one curriculum choice that will meet all of your needs. The choice of what to use and in what proportions they are used is going to have to be guided by you, your child, and your family. Don't be afraid to try out many different materials and continually reassess your choices. The more flexibility you have with this, the more successful your teaching endeavors will be.

7

Testing & Assessments:
How Does Your Child Stack Up?

After I had been homeschooling for about a year, I started to feel the need to have my son tested. I don't know where this urge came from; probably from a lack of confidence in what I was doing and the pressure to conform to standard kindergarten practices. I never questioned whether testing was useful or beneficial; I just researched educational psychologists in my area and then spent a small fortune getting a battery of tests run on my son. The results were disappointingly exactly what I had predicted. I had accurately pegged his strengths and weaknesses before he was tested.

In direct contrast to the above experience, a good homeschooling friend of mine had a son that was not doing well in anything she was trying to teach him, especially his reading. She was having a lot of frustration and finally in desperation took him to get tested. It turned out he had a learning disability called Visual Tracking Disorder[7] that was previously undiagnosed, and he has since benefited greatly from appropriate intervention. This mom was very pleased with her investment of time and money and found the information to be helpful and something she could not have figured out on her own.

The decision whether to formally test your children or to offer assessments as a part of regular lesson plans is complex. There is no one clear solution or answer to the question, "Should I test my child?"

Testing inherently involves comparisons. The prevalence of comparisons in our society was hammered home to me as I recently sat watching one of my daughter's soccer games. My daughter was with her team warming up while I was enjoying a few moments to work on a cross-stitch project before her game began. I found myself listening in on a conversation about the previous game that was taking place behind me. One mom gushed about how happy she was that her girl's team had won their game because it put them in the top rankings for their age group, and she watched the rankings closely every season to make sure her daughter's team stayed ahead. One of the dads fervently agreed, and the conversation continued in the same vein for several minutes. Not once did they call over their daughters and congratulate them on their performance or win. There was no mention of teamwork, sportsmanship, or having fun; the emphasis was solely upon beating the other team. The implied message was that winning was all that counted. Worse was the more subversive message implied in their discussion, that it was only necessary to do better than the others rather than to live up to one's potential.

We all like to win but it isn't everything. It certainly is a component of success, but there are others that are equally important, like personal satisfaction, trying your best, and teamwork. Kids in traditional schools realize early that they don't have to be the best they can be – just a little bit better than the next kid. When a child knows the answer to a question that nobody else does, they are praised and rewarded. But if they start to know too much and raise their hand for every answer they are chastised and told to allow the other kids to have a chance.

As a pediatrician, I was confronted with the issue of comparisons in every aspect of my work. Pediatrics is a field governed by norms. Growth and development are monitored and judged from birth all the way through puberty and adolescence. We're trained to spot children outside these norms in case there are serious underlying problems. This can be wonderful, as many childhood diseases are caught early and treatments begun at a time when the outcome can be significantly impacted, but norms can sometimes be stifling and counter-productive.

When considering a pre-set point of achievement, it's necessary to consider whether it's even a valid measuring point and indicator of success or mastery. Schools tend to set these measuring points based upon tests they give. Success is based upon how well a child can memorize and regurgitate facts for a test, not on true learning. For homeschoolers, it's important to set your own indicators of success for your children based upon what you want them to learn and retain.

The issues surrounding testing and assessments are complicated and difficult to answer. One of the first questions you need to answer is, what type of information do you want to find? The clearer the goals are when you start, the happier you will be with the outcome.

IQ Testing

IQ testing refers to the administration of a standardized test that will result in a number or "Intelligence Quotient" representing the innate cognitive ability of an individual.

The average person should score 100, with numbers above 100 meaning more intelligent than average and numbers below 100 vice versa. Most schools test students' IQ's sometime in the early elementary years, usually at kindergarten. Some IQ tests are better suited to discern lower intelligences and some can better assess certain strengths. If you decide to IQ test, it should be done with a qualified child psychologist that has clearly identified the best scenario for your child.

Many people question the benefit of knowing this "magic number." Often the IQ is not predictive of academic performance. There are many other factors that can lead to academic success, such as motivation, dedication, and persistence. I wanted to know the IQ of my children, but knowing the results hasn't helped me one bit in my curriculum choices or any other aspect of homeschooling. I confess, I had my kids tested purely to satisfy my curiosity.

The most compelling reason not to test is that there's usually not much information gained by it for the average child. However, there are a few instances in which it is necessary. Some special education programs require an IQ test score to qualify. Many of these programs can be helpful for parents in terms of resources, counseling, distance or local learning opportunities, and a social network of other parents experiencing similar issues with their children.

IQ testing is probably most beneficial for parents when they suspect their children to be outliers from norms. If you suspect your child might be on the fringes, then finding out where your child is on that spectrum will probably not cause you to change your teaching style or subjects covered, but it might help you refine your techniques or strategies. Also, the IQ test can help you gauge areas of relative strength. For example, if a child scores very high on the verbal subtest but low on the spatial reasoning, you might adjust the way certain materials are presented.

Communicating with children about their weaknesses can be dangerous, however. Some children are devastated by perceived failure, and it's hard for young minds to realize that weaknesses and failure are not the same. It's helpful to decide before the testing how and whether you will share the results and how you'll use them.

The question of whether or not to test IQ is one of the most common questions encountered when standardized testing is discussed in homeschooling circles. If you decide to pursue this testing, save up for it, as it can cost several thousand dollars. Make sure also that you research educational psychologists thoroughly before you jump in. You will want someone familiar with homeschooling at best and certainly one that specializes in children at the least. Also, make an appointment to meet them first before you bring your child in. You want to make sure they do not have any judgements about your educational choices for your child. Make sure you communicate your needs and expectations clearly before starting. This will save you money and may even bring more accurate results if the psychologist understands your goals before testing. Then after you have reached a comfort level with the psychologist, introduce your child to them and ensure their personalities mesh well and that your child feels comfortable.

Grade-Level Achievement Testing

Grade-level achievement tests are now almost universal in American schools, with most every state having their own minimum level skills tests that are given to all children in public schools. California has the STAR test, Florida the FCAT, and in Texas the TAAS. In fact as part of the No Child Left Behind Act all states were required to implement a system of testing certain subjects in certain specified grades. A lot is riding upon these test scores, including school funding and recruitment of teachers and administrators. Many school districts have made funding contingent upon rising test scores, so schools are extremely focused on raising their scores. While there are many problems with these standardized tests, they can be useful in certain circumstances.

If you're withdrawing your child from school, it's nice to know what they have mastered and what they have not. Even if you have already been homeschooling, sometimes you might have a question about a student's mastery of a subject or their readiness to proceed with a new subject. Usually the best reason to consider these is if you feel your child will be returning to a traditional school environment in the near future. It might just ease the transition to the school environment if the administration can accurately place your child in classes with other similarly scoring children.

One downside of achievement testing involves the cost and difficulty of arranging it. Usually the tests are administered by licensed and approved individuals and are scored by a central facility that takes weeks or even months to return the results. They are very expensive if you get them through an educational psychologist and if you go through a school system, you risk being put on the school's radar screen; most school districts are familiar with homeschoolers and understand and accommodate them, but for many, the risk that they might be harassed or pursued by the educational authorities is not worth the risk of a free test.

For children who have been homeschooling for a while, standardized tests aren't worth much. Most of these tests are scored based upon the scores of other test takers. If you administer this test and your child scores extremely low in math for example, it's likely that he or she has been learning other material. It could be just that the child was not ready for those concepts at that age or that you chose not to teach those subjects. Conversely, a child who scores very high in a certain subject area has probably been taught a lot in that area compared to traditionally schooled children.

The interpretation of the result of a grade-level standardized test is difficult at best for homeschoolers as I mentioned above and not that useful overall. If there are questions about achievement in a particular subject, it might be worthwhile to talk with a knowledgable child psychologist who could point you in the direction of other more specific tests.

College Preparatory Testing

College preparatory testing is one area where the decision on whether to test or not is taken out of your hands. Whether or not it's needed depends on your child's future goals and career path. Looking into the future can be frightening for some teens who don't have a clear idea about what they want to do in life. In these cases it's best to go ahead and prepare them to take these tests, because you never know when it might come up in the future.

By college preparatory testing, I am lumping together a bunch of different tests. The most popular are the PSAT, the SAT, the ACT, and the SAT II subject tests. The PSAT test is usually administered in tenth or eleventh grade and is used to determine National Merit Scholars. High school diploma equivalency exams can also be lumped in here because in some instances you can use these in place of a high school diploma.

The first thing to consider is what your child will need in the future. When investigating undergraduate education, look carefully at university admissions requirements. Many institutions require test scores on applications and will not even consider an applicant for admission without them. There are many institutions, however, that are becoming more friendly to homeschoolers and will allow a portfolio of work to be used instead. Some institutions that require test scores for freshman don't require them for transfer students. This can be helpful to students who finished their high school education early and go to community college before heading off to finish their degree at a four year university.

Obviously you can't anticipate every need, but be aware that you will have to provide some accountability for what your child has learned, whether that be in the form of test scores, a portfolio, or a transcript of college level classes at a community college.

Another important consideration is that homeschooled children are usually not as prepared in the mechanics of test taking. By the time traditionally schooled children take the SAT for example, they have had years of practice bubbling in their names and birth dates on forms. They are well-versed in test-taking etiquette and have started to develop their own test-taking strategies. Luckily, test taking is a skill that can be learned like any other. First, if you and your child decide to pursue this type of testing, get your hands on a test review book with a sample test in it. Also, try to visit the testing site beforehand to let your child become comfortable there. Consider a review course if you feel it necessary, and remember, all of these tests can be re-taken.

Assessing on an Ongoing Basis

Assessing on an ongoing basis really means testing your children the way schools do every so often on the material you have taught them. Deciding when, how, and even if you want to do this is more of an art than a science. Curricula-in-a-box usually come with tests and a recommended schedule for administering them, and some textbooks and workbooks have chapter tests or unit tests dispersed through the book. For less traditional curricula, you will have to be more creative about where to get your assessment materials from, if you decide to administer some. There are a variety of ways to obtain assessments for subject matter mastery, including resources on the web from primary education up to college level sources that post their tests or samples for public use.

There are other methods of determining whether a subject has been mastered without a formal test. Many times practical life application is a powerful tool to test and to reinforce the necessity of learning certain subjects. For example, my son wanted a pirate-themed birthday party several years ago, and I told him that was fine – if he did the math while we bought supplies. He had to multiply, divide, add, and subtract to figure out if there were going to be enough supplies, stay within the budget, and fill the goody bags. I saw real fast that we needed way more practice on our multiplication tables!

Another strong method of assessing knowledge involves narration. If children have truly mastered and incorporated knowledge, they will be able to repeat it and explain it to another. This is great if you have more than one child, but you can also engage grandparents, friends, neighbors, or your non-homeschooling spouse. Alternatively, if you like keeping a journal of a child's work, they could write a paragraph about what they learned. This is a great way to incorporate writing skills and can mature with your child very easily. In the elementary years it will be primarily just a regurgitation of facts but as the child matures and gets into middle and high school, their narrations should start to make connections and draw inferences.

I once taught a science class to a few homeschooled children at the behest of their parents. Some of the children were all for a final exam and eagerly anticipated the opportunity to show off their knowledge, while others wanted to drop out if they were required to take a test. I realized that this subject of on-going assessing was just as individual as everything else in homeschooling. There is no one right answer or for-mula to use.[9] I recommend asking the following questions of yourself and your children before making any decisions about tests.

1. How will your children react if they do well or don't do well? Will not doing well motivate them to do better or will it demoralize them?
2. What level of mastery do you consider appropriate? Will you insist on 100 percent mastery or do you believe in some leeway?
3. Can you as a teacher be comfortable with administering assessments? Do you need those scores as an external validation of your effort?

The last question hits many people especially hard. There's nothing wrong with needing test scores as an external validation of your efforts, but understand that that is what they are for. If you don't feel that your children need assessments but you do, are there other ways you can meet your needs?

Central to the whole idea of homeschooling is preparing your children for life, and there are very few formal tests in life. There are many homeschooled children who are regularly assessed and there are an equal number who will go through their whole lives without a single assessment being administered. As long as the process is tailored to the individual child and family there really isn't any wrong answer.

PART 3:
Highlighting the Homeschooling Lifestyle

8

Successful Homeschooling Households

Let me describe a typical trip to the grocery store in my fantasyland. My children and I would take along note cards of common foods written in a foreign language – let's say French – so that we could learn our vocabulary as we strolled the aisles. After a time, our conversation would gently transition into a meaningful discussion about good nutrition, food labeling, and the vagaries of advertising. The kids would be actively involved in picking items for well-balanced meals, and we might practice the previous week's math lessons while in line to check out. We'd step out into a sunny day with smiles on our faces and load up the car with particularly springy steps.

Ha. Now let me tell you what really happens. Usually by the time we get to the store, everyone is so ravenous that none of the decisions are made with a rational mind. The kids start the minute we enter the store with, "Can we get a big bag of [X candy]? Why can't we have [sugary and brightly colored cereal]? It tastes really good!" I have a list in the bottom of my purse that never sees the light of day. When my kids were smaller, I would put them in the cart and dash through the store down the middle of the aisles so the kids' hands could touch as little as possible, because if I didn't, they would pick random items off the shelf and throw them in the basket. I usually don't know exactly what I've purchased until we unpack it at home. We're lucky if we get half of what's on the list, and "well-balanced" isn't quite the descriptor I would apply.

There are times when day-to-day activities seem difficult to the homeschooling parent. How is it possible to run your household efficiently and educate your children at the same time? Well, rest assured, it can be done and in fact is probably easier than you think. There are many things that successful homeschooling families do to keep their households running smoothly without compromising any other goals they have.

I know many of you are thinking, "I can't even keep up with cleaning now and I send my kids to school, so how will I do it when they are home all the time?" Well, let's break running a household down into two parts: errands outside of the house and cleaning and cooking inside the house. I will show you how to address each of these areas while homeschooling and even how each of these can enhance your homeschooling.

Errands Outside the House

Most parents who don't homeschool run errands while their kids are in school, letting them accomplish their errands in a peaceful and organized manner. As tempting as that sounds, we as homeschoolers can lose teachable moments and learning opportunities if we start longing for that freedom. Many of the most important skills in life are never taught in school, such as interacting with a wide variety of people (rather than just the ones of your age or socioeconomic background), working with banks, paying bills, making investments, buying homes, prioritizing goals, balancing work-life issues, and running a household. As well, real life shows children the practical application of their schoolwork.

Also, any moment we are not with our children means there might be situations that we are missing in their life. When I was in private practice, I saw a myriad of physical complaints that had their roots not in physical problems, but anxieties and fears. The most common one of these were stomach aches manifesting in the morning before kids left for school. Usually after all physical causes were ruled out, we were still left scratching our heads as to what was the root cause. Many times, the children themselves couldn't tell us. During the school day, something was usually happening that made the child anxious or nervous, whether it was the dread of a particular class, bullying in the lunchroom, or a fear of getting up in front of the class to present a project. Sometimes if these were really egregious situations, the children could voice their particular worries to myself or their parents, but more often than not, if they were less severe, the child themselves wouldn't even be able to make the connection between the anxiety-causing problem and the physical complaint. Kids do not place importance on events that we as adults would recognize as a difficult situation. It was simply that they didn't fully recognize the problem, or it was forgotten in the frenzy of a normal day's activities.

To adults, this can seem ridiculous, but there is a complex interplay between reluctance to confront authority, social fear or acceptance, and a desire to please adults. There is not really a need to *change* these behaviors as they are a part of the make-up of childhood, but instead to *recognize* them and *accommodate* them. This understanding will allow us to prevent situations in which worries or concerns might be subjugated and make sure they are addressed in a timely and appropriate fashion. If you are present with your children, these situations will not crop up, allowing you to address them immediately and bypass any ongoing problems that can occur.

If you do not already try to incorporate your kids in everything you do, consider starting. Each day, look at what you have to do and try to arrange it so your kids can go with you. When times are tough and you swear you're going to hunt me down for suggesting this, focus on why they're with you. What lessons are they learning? What life skill can they take away from the interaction? What about the situation can you turn into a learning experience?

The inevitable will happen, though. Just when you feel comfortable taking the kids somewhere, or on your very first try, they will suddenly sprout horns and become little devils. Kids will be kids, and we should understand that. Creative techniques can help them learn to obey and listen when needed, but we should not feel guilty for having our kids with us, or worse, bend to popular opinion and leave our kids on the periphery. Children and parents together compose the basic family unit, and if it takes a little noise to keep the family unit together, then let it be and be proud of it.

🔌 Once, when my kids were two and five, we were shopping at the grocery store. They were cranky and nasty, and I wasn't feeling much better. Nothing I could do seemed to help matters at all. No amount of cajoling, bribery, or threatening seemed to improve. I told them, "One more word out of either one of you, and you will be sorry." The next time they fussed, I turned around, put the cold items back, and took the cart up to the front. I gave it to a bag boy and apologized but said we had to leave the store. I took the kids by their hands, walked out of the store, got in the car and drove away. There was absolute silence on the way home. Dinner that night was meager indeed since we didn't get any new food, but they learned a lesson without me getting upset or yelling. Now whenever they're difficult while we shop, I just remind them about that experience.

If this is a new concept for you, start slowly. Kids that have not been habitually included will resist at first. Don't worry that they are resisting you or your ideas. They are creatures of habit too, and they need time to adjust to change. Make sure you emphasize to your children the importance of their inclusion. Explain to them in detail what you are accomplishing and your reasons for it.

For example, if your errands include a bank, do not assume your children understand anything about banks. Take the time to point out things to them they might not notice, like the security cameras. Let them fill out deposit or withdrawal slips. Explain to them about bank statements, checkbooks and balancing an account. If you are going to a dry cleaners, explain to them the difference between dry cleaning and laundering yourself at home. If you have to go to the post office, talk about stamp collecting, discuss the art and designs of stamps, or show them the different ways to track mail.

TIPS AND TRICKS FOR RUNNING ERRANDS WITH KIDS

Consider the age and interest level of your children: Even for the best behaved young child, it will be hard to be strapped in the car for a long period of time. Try to look at your week in advance and see where you can group errands or combine them. Maybe several shorter days will be more successful than one long day.

Keep the children fed: I know this sounds basic, but a full tummy is a happy one. You can often get one more errand squeezed in after a snack.

Keep a supply of interesting books, games, or other activities available: This is especially important when your errands might involve a wait, whether it's in a line at a grocery store or at a doctor's office. Make sure you change these regularly to keep the interest level up.

Develop a special something for certain errands: This is especially good if you have a recurrent place to go that involves long waits. The orthodontist became our bailiwick years ago. I started in braces after the birth of my daughter and the monthly visits soon became onerous for the children. I usually was in pain after the adjustments and dealing with whining children was not high on my list. I usually never allow the kids fast food, but after the orthodontist visits I instituted a policy of taking them for a milkshake after the visits if they were well-behaved. They started to love the orthodontist office and became very well-behaved. (I also liked this system because milkshakes were about all I could eat after

---

the visits.) This has continued to this day. With both of my children in braces now, they still look forward to the milkshake they know is waiting for them after a visit to the orthodontist.

As adults who are used to doing things in America's frenetic manner, remember that children do not understand or comprehend without explanation. They will learn of course by example, but it would be a true crime not to encourage full understanding of what they are doing or seeing. A perfect example is swiping credit cards at payment machines. Kids will know it has to be done to pay, but unless you explain about the magnetic strip on the back of cards and the process by which data is stored on it, they will not truly understand it. This will push your knowledge as a parent, causing you to have to research things if you don't already know them. This type of knowledge and questioning is one of the most important aspects of a life-long education. It will develop critical thinking skills and foster a questioning nature that will be less easily swayed or convinced as an adult.

Invariably questions will come up that you can't answer – make sure you keep a note pad and pencil in your bag to jot these down. Before you know it, both you and your children will be looking forward to going out, even for the most routine of errands, and you will be amazed at how well-behaved they are and how fun it is to have them with you. By discussing these topics, not only will you be teaching your children valuable life lessons, you will be taking the drudgery out of your life. Errands can be boring and repetitive, but start looking for new and interesting things around you, and you will be amazed at what you see and what you can learn.

Cooking and Cleaning

When you're getting things done at home, it's marginally easier because you don't have to worry about making everyone presentable.

Nevertheless, figuring out when to mop the kitchen floor or clean the bathroom can still seem like an insurmountable task. However the flip side is that because you spend a lot more time at home than many other people, you have to have some semblance of order and peace to be able to accomplish everything you want. You don't have the luxury of walking out the door every morning and shutting the mess out of your life for the day.

There are really two issues at stake here. The first is the clutter issue and the second is the cleaning issue. Clutter is a hard one. It seems the universe has endorsed a law of nature that states that the amount of junk strewn around a house is inversely proportional to the amount of learning that has occurred in the past four hours. When my husband comes home and finds a neat house with everything in its place, I can guarantee that nobody learned much that day. The days it looks like a bomb has gone off in the house are usually the days that I remember because tons of learning took place. When the kids are excited about a topic or school work, I find it counterproductive to stop them and insist we clean up. We move from one subject to another, waiting to put things away until a time when they are not engaged or interested.

   ♠ A good friend of mine who has three kids developed an ingenious system of toy rotation to help solve the problem of the clutter and mess her kids generate. She bought a bunch of large storage containers and grouped the toys; for example, action figures in one, trains in one, dolls in one, etc. Each child got to pick one container at a time to play with, and every week or so they would clean that container up, put it away, and bring out another. If a container went unused for a year, it was sold at a garage sale. The mother remarked to me that when certain toys were put away for a period of time and then brought back, the kids played with them more, whereas when they were always available, the kids fussed they had nothing to play with.

One of my homeschooling friends is adamant about the necessity of having a cleaning crew come in and do the heavy cleaning work. She says that even though it is a drain on the budget, it frees her up for more value-added tasks around the house. Another friend feels just the opposite and likes to clean when she and her family have the time and the need.

I've been in both places at different points in my homeschooling career. There have been times when cleaning the house by myself has been impossible and I've needed help, but there have been other times when life has made it possible to take care of things myself, and sometimes with less trouble than working with a cleaning service.

If you choose to go without, remember you have built in help at home. Even the tiniest children can help, and often love it when they are included. One trick I learned from another mom was the term "ten second tidy." It was made popular by a kids' TV show called *The Big Comfy Couch* in which the main character would rush around cleaning up for ten seconds at the end of the show. Of course, anyone who only needs a ten-second tidy to get their house in order should be nominated for sainthood, but the idea is still good. I've found it helpful to have a ten-second tidy right before walking out the door to get in the car. When everyone's rushing, it's amazing to see how much gets done: I can get the dishwasher mostly emptied, the kitchen counter cleared off, or a bed made in this time. And if everybody is doing it, the efforts add up. Kids will rush to do this style of cleaning before they go out because they know it's a time-limited task and there's something to do afterwards.

In addition to housecleaning, there are countless other tasks to accomplish in the course of a day to keep our households running smoothly, and as the parent at home, the burden usually falls on the shoulders of the primary homeschooling parent. There are things however that can be done to make your days easier and allow you to accomplish things you need to do even with your children around you 24/7.

Getting things done will became significantly easier if you start assigning a prescribed playtime to your children every day. At first they won't believe you, but soon they will catch on. Many times when adults are not actively engaging children, they will mope around and not be very constructive. There tends to be complaining about the fact that "there's nothing to do." Free-play is a very important skill for children to have and one that's not particularly valued by traditional school systems who have to be accountable for almost every minute of a child's day.

When you start to assign a play period each day, make sure to give it rules and guidelines, such as no computers or video games, and encourage your children to take toys out they haven't played with in a long while. When I started doing this with my kids, they thought this was the coolest; when else has the evil schoolmaster mom told them to go play?

In this same vein, once your children are independent readers, you can assign a reading time every day. They should be able pick anything they want to read, even a comic book, as long as they are quiet and reading. They will be thrilled they get to pick something, and think it is fun, while you will get quiet time to do what you need to and have the satisfaction that the children are engaging in an activity that will benefit them.

TIPS AND TRICKS FOR GETTING THE CLEANING AND COOKING DONE

Quiet/Reading/Play Time: As I described above, having dedicated time for these activities will allow you free time to tackle the necessary duties around the house.

Pace Yourself: Look at the cleaning as a continuum over a week's time. I know this has the potential for being depressing, since at the end of the week, you will just have to start over again, but it will help to break the job down into manageable parts day by day, giving you a sense of accomplishment and progress each day.

Recruit Help: Even the smallest child can help, as can the non-home-schooling spouse. Do not be afraid to ask for help and assigning appropriate tasks. Anything that you can remove from your plate will make the overall household tasks easier to accomplish.

Cooking: Enlist help with the cooking and train them young! Especially for breakfast, teaching your children to pour their own bowl of cereal or make toast can allow you to start your day with some necessary tasks be fore facing the children. Also, having a pizza night or something similar with quick pick-up food will help take the pressure off dinner preparation for one night of the week at least. The kids will also look forward to this if you hype it up as something special. Cooking in bulk when you do cook will help save time by creating left-overs.

Don't sweat: If your house is messy or the dishes are piling up, just start small and don't try to tackle everything at once. There's nothing to be gained from a tired, frantic homeschooling parent that is too frazzled to teach.

A lot of getting your household chores done comes down to deciding what really needs to be done and what can be done without. Once you have pared it down to the bare minimum, creativity can really help in figuring out ways to accomplish your tasks. When you are stressed for time and feel you can't even get the smallest things accomplished, it's time for a breather and some self-affirmation. It takes a lot to be in charge of your child's education, and it's okay for some things to slide.

9

The Homeschool Bus

Not long ago, as the children and I spent a day shuffling from one activity to another, I realized we were a tad over-scheduled. We started out the day with an orthodontist appointment for my daughter, then had to race like mad to get to my son's violin and music theory lesson. Then it was a quick rush home to get ready for the science club hosted at my house every Thursday, followed by a trip to the acting class that started a half hour after science club was over. By evening, all three of us were exhausted and frazzled. I felt like a bus driver speeding a group of tourists through the sites of a homeschooling day; there was always another place to be.

I'm not alone in this affliction. It is all too common a phenomenon among homeschoolers even though there comes a point when it somewhat defeats the purpose of homeschooling, which is to be flexible, adaptable, and able to take advantage of the teachable moments. We somehow feel that because we have those hours during the school day free, we can schedule ourselves to the breaking point.

The false belief that this is a good thing comes from a couple different places. First, homeschooling parents feel the pressure of being responsible for every aspect of their children's education. It's a big responsibility and overscheduling is a common form of overcompensation. Second, homeschoolers see two parts to education: theory and application. Classes often don't seem complete without a hands-on extension of what we teach from curricula. Homeschoolers aren't content to teach their children in the narrow confines of their home; we zealously augment the book-learning with enrichment activities designed to give children a more well-rounded experience and fuller understanding of the subjects we teach.

Depending on your homeschooling style, extracurricular activities will have differing levels of importance in your day, but no matter what kind of homeschooler you are, enrichment activities are central to every homeschooler's curriculum. They can be wonderful and invaluable additions to your homeschool experience, but they do come at a price that needs to be recognized and accounted for. Not only do you need to consider each particular child's needs for enrichment, you have to consider the needs of the rest of the family and the organizations you are committing your child to. This chapter will focus on those regularly scheduled enrichment activities that have a more structured timetable. I'll tackle enrichment activities that are less structured, such as road trips, and one-time trips like museums and field trips, in the next chapter.

Being over-scheduled can be stressful for the whole family and can lead to resentment and poor performance. When we find ourselves pulled in too many directions, it can lead to us forgetting our overall mission statement and our own needs. I recommend taking a large monthly calendar and adding the activities you already are committed to and that you feel strongly about and enjoy. Don't forget things that impact the whole family, such as church, work schedules, or exercise. If it takes some time and organization, it needs to be written down. Once all of these activities are on the calendar, pencil in the time you devote to learning and time for free play. Do not feel that these should be added only Monday through Friday.

After this, step back down and look at what you have. If some days look heinous, consider what you can change or modify to ease your burden. After I did this calendar exercise, I was amazed at how many times a week our family was in the orthodontist, dentist, doctor's or veterinarian's office. I since have moved all appointments to Wednesday mornings. It has greatly simplified my life in that now I am accustomed to Wednesday mornings being early mornings out. I rarely if ever forget appointments anymore. I also rescheduled my daughter's guitar lessons to occur on the same day as my son's violin lessons, so the whole family knows that Tuesdays are for music (and the library, since it happens to be close). Everybody knows to grab musical instruments, sheet music, and library books on the way out the door on Tuesdays.

What Kinds of Activities to Look For

When considering how and what to add into your homeschooling experience, there are a couple of key factors that will help guide the process. The first thing to consider when planning your child's activities is their interest. No amount of cajoling will make an activity successful if your child is not engaged in it. What are their interests and passions? What can you not help them with? When my son wanted to play the violin, I signed him up for lessons because I know nothing about the violin, but when my daughter wanted to learn to play the guitar, I was slower to do so because I played the guitar as a teenager. I started teaching her on my own, and then I signed her up for lessons after she outgrew my beginner knowledge.

Many homeschoolers look for PE classes or sport teams so their children can get a group sport experience. Another subject many homeschoolers look for in a group experience is science. It can be done alone, but is a little easier and less expensive with a group because it's hard to find and maintain the necessary ingredients for experiments on hand. I have to laugh about this because I never seem to have the right ingredients in my house when they're called for in a science experiment. If you read many of these experiments they will say, "common household goods only," but then when you read the individual experiments you find that you will need alum, liquid starch, and a pie tin. Unfortunately, none of those items I have or can readily get except for the pie tin, which if I had one, would have been purchased for a specific reason and already used.

Art is another subject frequently taught outside the home because of the availability and cost of materials. Be careful not to reflexively add every class that looks good, though. Too often parents assume they need help without really considering the facts. Many of these subjects can be taught at home quite successfully.

There are art programs that can be purchased as well as complete science kits that have instructions and all the necessary materials. While these do tend to be expensive, sometimes they are less so than the aggravation of getting to and from a scheduled class. It really depends on what you and your children are looking for in an experience and how much you all are looking for a group versus an individual experience.

Places to Look for Enrichment Activities

Many businesses have sprung up to cater to parents of traditionally schooled children, who often look for ways to schedule their children's time after school. One major benefit of establishments like these is their child-friendly setup. The staff is used to children and usually the schedule of snacks and bathroom breaks and the overall facilities are geared towards accommodating children. However, these places often present major scheduling problems for homeschooling parents who like to use the afternoon or evening for schoolwork, or that travel and have unpredictable schedules. Often these establishments operate on a school-year calendar, require payments on a monthly or quarterly schedule, and enforce strict policies about things like making up missed classes. This is a nightmare for those of us who like to be more free and easy with our schedules.

If the establishment is willing, oftentimes a special homeschooling class can be held during the day to better accommodate homeschooler's needs. This can be great if you have a group of kids and parents willing to start a class with you. If this is not the case, you are stuck having to put your child in with the masses. The best attitude to adopt in this situation is just one of being a good-will ambassador for homeschooling. Explain your scheduling needs to the staff and ask how flexible they can be with you. Often, when you explain up front, the staff will work with homeschoolers and allow us to be less rigid. But when they won't, just accept that you will not usually get the full value out a class and assuage yourself with the knowledge that your kids are still better off.

There are many places to look for classes for your children to take. Most cities have a community services department or a department of parks and recreation that will offer classes to a variety of age levels and in a variety of topics. These usually are fairly reasonable in price. Also, local teen centers, YMCA's, and libraries often have classes to choose from. If you live near a performing arts center or civic center, check out their offerings. There are also often local businesses that will offer courses, such as culinary centers, sports stores, and zoos to name a few.

 HOMESCHOOLING HIGHLIGHT

Many parents are concerned about whether their children will matriculate well with children from a traditional schooling background. There might be trepidation about making friends. However, this is rarely a problem with homeschoolers. They are so well socialized that there are usually no problems with integration, especially since these classes are grouped by interests.

If you have a particular need for a certain class and have not been able to locate one that fits with your schedule or budget, consider setting up one on your own. For very little money, professionals or advanced students will usually be willing to teach a class to either just your children or a group of homeschoolers.

A fellow homeschooling family I know had quite an interest in the Harry Potter books and the children wanted to continue with the magic sparked by the books. The mom started a class on the wizard world with each session focusing on a different aspect of this world. One class was a Flourish and Blotts class, where the children learned about writing implements through the ages, calligraphy, and made their own quills. Another was all about names and the author's choice of names of characters and what they meant. The children kept journals, were assigned to houses, and earned points for their houses. It was a great success and had the children engaged and excited.

Warning Label

While these enrichment classes can be wonderful additions to round out a homeschooling curriculum, there are some considerations that homeschoolers should be aware of before diving in. Most establishments offering scheduled, child-oriented activities owe their very existence to children from traditional schools and may in some ways mimic schools structures by being somewhat more stratified and hierarchical than many homeschoolers would like. For some, this won't matter, but there are some homeschoolers who shun this structure, or children who do not function well with these constraints. The fact that many of these organizations operate just like traditional schools needs to be taken into account when enrolling your child in one of these classes. In a way I feel like a pediatrician here in much the same way I would warn parents about the side effects of certain medications. None of the reasons I present are enough to shun group classes, it just pays to be aware and informed at the beginning and be able to set appropriate expectations.

Even if you can get a group of homeschoolers together for a class, the staff still operates the same, so it might be worthwhile spending some time around the staff explaining the differences they will see when dealing with homeschooled students. They will automatically assume that children of outlying ages will not be able to function well, causing an automatic exclusion of children below or above their posted age limits as a knee jerk reflex. If you feel your children outside of their age limitations would still benefit from the activity, it will be up to you to convince them.

The staff also will not understand that homeschooling children by and large aren't socialized into a classroom environment. Our homeschooled children will not automatically raise their hands before asking a question, use the restroom only at scheduled breaks, or be able to line up easily by height when asked. You can rest assured, however, even though your children may not be able to do these things, they will not be hampered in life, as none of these are really important skills.

I have been in a situation before where the teacher of a class of homeschooled students was angered by the fact that the students were so inquisitive and thought their questioning of what he was teaching was undermining his authority. (I felt that he was only worried the kids would expose his weaknesses in understanding, but I obviously couldn't say that.) I have also run into problems where the teachers were expecting a certain level of competency across the board in the students (after all, that is what schools produce) and was in a dither to find that some kids were well above and some were below their expectations. Typically, by their design and very nature these programs are not very flexible as they are many times just an extension of traditional school.

🔔 For example, I signed my homeschooled girl scout troop up for a workshop designed specifically for Brownie Girl Scouts at a local botanic garden. The docent of the park was an older gentleman who had brought a worksheet designed by the park staff for the girls to complete as part of the badge work. He could not get his mind wrapped around the fact that we had some 3rd grade age children that could not write and others that were well beyond what he was teaching. He was stuck on the fact that the girls had to fill out his worksheet and no other in order to get credit. This poor man was getting more and more frustrated and just stood there wringing his hands. Finally the parents took pity on him and stepped in.

Within seconds we had it all sorted out and he was smiling again. All we did was to tell the girls who couldn't write to draw pictures instead, and for those that needed more information and enrichment, we made sure they got some extra instruction. All the kids had a fun time and they all learned. Nobody felt uncomfortable with their performance, which might have happened if we hadn't stepped in.

It's wise to acquaint the staff that will be working with a group of homeschoolers with some of these basic tenets of homeschooling. It also helps to warn them to be flexible. Usually when warned, they will be able to adapt to the needs of the students, but it pays to watch closely. You do not want all your hard work to be undermined by the comments of a misinformed but well-meaning teacher.

You should be aware of these facts, depending on your goals for homeschooling. Remember back to the mission statement you wrote? This is an excellent time to review that. If you want to steer your children away from learning about the latest fashion trend, TV show, or rock band, think twice about putting your child into a group setting. All it takes is one exposure and your carefully constructed walls could come crumbling down.

Many people who criticize the sequestering nature of homeschooling will use this argument to make their point. They will automatically assume that by wanting to control the education that your children receive, whether it's academic or social, you are improperly sheltering them from life. Don't let them bother you. We all know that no matter how much we try to shelter our kids, at some point they will have to join the world. It's just that we as homeschoolers want control over when that will happen. If avoiding some of these things are important to you, think carefully about enrolling your child in a class full of other traditionally schooled children.

One craze I was particularly adamant about avoiding with my children was Pokémon. I was lucky in the fact that without television, my kids were not exposed at home. For several years while this fad was at its height, I avoided any sort of group gathering for my children where it was possible that subject might have been introduced. They totally missed the hysteria and I felt very happy that I had managed to orchestrate it. Later on, when they did take group classes, my son heard about Pokémon for the first time. He asked a few questions about it and after he learned more, he declared it dumb. I felt so vindicated. By waiting until he was a little bit older, I was able to deflect something that otherwise might have had an influence on him. Of course, there are other people that do not share this opinion about Pokémon, but the concept is the same. We can and should have control over what our children are exposed to.

Your reaction to these group learning experiences will depend to a great extent on your own children and educational philosophies, but hopefully I've opened your eyes to some of the things to watch out for. Not all of these are bad but they need to be recognized and anticipated.

Successful Outcomes

In order to have the best possible experiences with your children and their extracurricular activities, there are several things you can do at the beginning. First, make sure you don't overschedule yourself. The best classes in the world will not mean anything if you are rushing around and going crazy trying to get to them.

Next, think of your child's learning styles when planning extracurricular activities. If your child is a kinesthetic learner and needs to move around in order to learn, a science class at a local community college may not be the way to go. This situation might call for an outdoors science class at a local park. If they're not morning people, even if it's the opportunity of a lifetime, a class at eight a.m. will not benefit your children.

Don't forget your needs or those of your family either. Getting to and from these activities can be time consuming and tough especially if you have other children who need to come along for the ride but aren't participating in the activity. If you find yourself spending a lot of time in a car, consider audiobooks. At other times, take a moment to share a story about your childhood. Kids love hearing about their parents at the same age and sometimes it's hard to take the time to do this at home.

Save certain activities for the car or when you're waiting at one activity with another child. Last year, my son accomplished his Propositional Logic work in the car as he and I sat outside a music studio while my daughter took guitar lessons. It was a great forty-five minutes of concentrated time without other distractions. I would turn off my cell phone and we would work on his exercises while we waited. In fact, once when we missed a lesson because my daughter was sick and I pulled the logic book out at home, he looked at me like I was crazy.

Enrichment activities can be a great way to introduce children to some experiences that they would not otherwise have, providing great hands on experience that's sometimes hard to provide for your children on your own. These classes can be valuable learning extensions when chosen correctly and their impact carefully considered.

10

On the Road

In the previous chapter I discussed enrichment activities that were of a more "classroom" type and scheduled nature. These can be wonderful extensions to your curriculum, but the strength of homeschooling lies in its freedom from schedules. Capturing those teachable moments often requires flexibility and freedom.

🔔 When my son was seven, he developed quite an interest in submarines and naval equipment. When this interest popped up, I immediately set about satisfying his curiosity. It didn't take long for us to run out of resources in our local library. There just wasn't very much material that was suitable for a child of his age. I researched on the internet and found that Kings Bay, Georgia was the home of the Trident submarine program of the US Navy. It wasn't too far away from us in Florida, so off we went. The town where the base was located had quite a few interesting museums and hands-on exhibits we took advantage of and we spent a fun week there satisfying his need for knowledge about submarines.

The ability to experience diversity and culture in person and learn about things with all your senses is one of the most valuable educational opportunities homeschooling offers. Traveling can mesh with any homeschooling style, budget, and subject. These flexible enrichment experiences can augment learning at any age level. Traveling with children, especially small ones, can take a little more planning, but the lessons last a lifetime. In this chapter, I will cover homeschool travel from the shortest day trips to more extensive road trips.

Day Trips

Day trips are a great way to incorporate enrichment into your homeschool experience. They're a good starting point if you're new to traveling as an educational pursuit or if other circumstances prevent longer travel. These trips can be as simple or as complex as you want to make them, from one or two hours to all-day excursions, depending on your wishes or needs. Some people will even set aside one day a week or a month that they reserve for these kinds of field trips. Scheduling these trips is a great way to encourage getting out, especially if it is not a focus of your daily life. I tend to be more of a homebody and would not normally pick up and take off, so scheduling a particular day of the week (Friday) to do this helps me find the motivation to keep this very important part of my curriculum current.

Start close to home. Many cities have a chamber of commerce website that you can access for ideas on activities. These trips are perfect for doing all the local things that most locals never get around to doing. Local parks sometimes have nature centers, trails, and interpretive signs that we rarely stop to look at. Museums, art galleries, city or town halls, police stations, water-treatment plants, recycling centers, and many other places usually have programs set up for school-aged children. If you're a member of an active homeschooling group, many times these field trips are arranged by the group and you can attend as a "school group." Most of these institutions welcome homeschoolers and will give them the same tours and opportunities as children in traditional school.

Some parents find themselves possessed of children who don't like to go out. They are content to sit curled up with a book or video game all day and never poke their nose out the door. For these children, start small and tailor the outing to their interests. If they like books, find a local author's club, poetry reading, or printing press that can give them a tour. If they like video games, see if there are any computer companies around or fancy arcades.

If you have a sports obsessed child, try to find a local sports team or college team that's playing near you. Kids that are interested in art might enjoy an art show. These are all ideas that you probably already do in your "free time," but now discuss them with the added distinction of being "school" oriented. When you start out with something they like, your children will not believe you mean for it to be an educational experience, but with a little encouragement, you can get lots of learning out of these trips.

The best tip to a successful day trip differs very little from ensuring success at anything else – plan on everything going wrong and try to be prepared for it. Early risers will do better with morning outings. No amount of excitement will stimulate good feelings in a late sleeping family that has to get up and out of the house by six am to reach somewhere.

TIPS AND TRICKS FOR SUCCESSFUL DAY TRIPS

1. Make sure you know where you're going. Getting lost is a bummer, especially when you're alone with kids.
2. Make sure someone knows where you're going and when you're expected to return.
3. Always start with a full tank of gas, money in your wallet, and a full charge on your cell phone.
4. Keep a container in the back of your car with a change of clothing for each child, plastic cups and a bottle of water, inexpensive jackets,

---

plastic silverware, sunscreen, a plastic potty (if your kids are of the potty training age), baby wipes, and a game or two. Obviously given the ages of your kids this list will have to be modified as needed, but these are just a few suggestions. I know the plastic silverware will raise eyebrows, but I can't tell you the number of times I've needed to eat in the car with the kids and haven't had the proper utensils. Invariably when we visit a drive-thru, I'm missing some sort of needed utensil.

5. Replace what you use from your emergency kit in the car. If you needed something once, chances are you'll need it again.

Traveling

Traveling for many families is vacation time and is treasured for relaxation and fun. However, homeschoolers have discovered traveling as an educational goal, involving a different focus than traveling for vacation and fun. That isn't to say that they can't coincide at times, but it's hard to combine a purely educational effort with other family members that are there for R&R. The educational benefits of traveling are manyfold. Imagine learning about the civil war and touring battlefields as an adjunct, or learning about ancient Rome and then visiting the ruins. These are grandiose ideas, but the benefits can even be seen in smaller trips such as learning about marine life and visiting the local aquarium, or learning about an artist and then touring several art museums. Even for children who have predominantly one learning style, traveling and getting to experience education in a multi-faceted way will cement the lessons in their heads. Being able to see, hear, touch, and in some cases smell the lessons will benefit any child and extend the learning opportunities.

All of these goals for learning are very different from the "vacation" mentality. It's hard to let this mentality go, but once you do it, you'll start to look at traveling as a vital and indispensable part of your home-schooling curriculum.

For starters, your preparations are different. You'll need to do some research ahead of time and pack relevant books, magazines, and other learning aids. You'll also need supplies for work along the way, including pens and pencils, pencil sharpeners, markers or crayons, journals, folders, scissors, glue, and any other supplies that you might make use of. There will not be much time for purely "fun" activities, like swimming in the hotel pool, miniature golf, and movies (although there will be some down time). Instead, you'll linger at museums, sketch in your journals at a park, or read to the kids about something they saw or will see on the trip. The rewards of this type of travel are immense. You'll find yourself lingering in places that before you would have sped by.

First, get a big map. This will give you a good overview of the trip. It really won't give you enough detail to make many plans, but it's important to help the kids get the big picture of what they will be embarking on.

There will be some things that will need to be decided on at the beginning, especially if you will be visiting friends and family along the way. (Usually they like to know when to expect their guests.) Don't be afraid to mark up the map with ideas or possibilities. The ideas you start out with will rarely be the ones you finish with. Big trips are generally fluid and apt to change depending on things like the weather, travel fatigue, finances, and new information.

Many people might shy away from this type of travel if they have large families or children who are at very different levels, age or interest-wise. These scenarios can make travel a little more challenging, but they're certainly not reasons to abandon traveling as an adjunct to the curriculum altogether. Both of these scenarios mean that you'll have to accommodate more people and activities. Consider combining trips to keep your broader audience happy. If you have one child who's studying American history that you are hoping to augment and another who's crazy about dinosaurs, make sure you find some natural history museums at your destinations. Consider talking about what was known about dinosaurs in different time periods and how perceptions of them changed with time.

There will be times where you have some children just left out. This can happen at the extremes of age – either the very young or the older teens who have already learned the material. For the younger children, don't fret. Even though it feels like you're just dragging them around, they'll absorb more than you think. And when you get to teaching them about the subject (even if it's years later) you can refer to the trip and drag out pictures and the journals your other children made. For older children who may have already learned about the subjects you're exploring, consider trying to bring a new subject into play. For example, if they've already studied the Civil War, introduce some philosophy of war or comparisons of the battles fought there versus other time periods in history. You can ask them to compare great generals from the Civil War and the ancient past. Pose questions to them like, "What would Caesar have done at this battle?"

A big consideration is the financial impact of the trip. Many homeschoolers maintain primary residences with bills to be paid and long trips incur their own expenses on top of already existing financial obligations. There are several things you can do though to affect the other areas that are under your control. There are ways to conserve money on a trip and operate off a budget.

One of the biggest expenses is lodging. Campgrounds are usually cheaper than hotels, but for a lone parent with one or more children, more than a night or two of camping can be extremely difficult. Hotels are sometimes an easier option that can be accommodated on just about any budget. First, when in an expensive market consider staying a little further away from city center and using public transportation to get around. Also, look at the time of week. Many expensive markets are cheaper during the weekend when business travelers are not around. There are also certain times of year in many markets that will have lower rates.

Before traveling, pick two or three chains and join their rewards program. This way, you can accumulate points or whatever other freebies they offer and try to use them along the way. Make promises to yourself about where you can stay and what kind of price point you're comfortable with. Sometimes it's hard to stick to these preconceptions but it will help you keep an eye on your lodging costs.

Make sure to chose hotels that have interior corridors for safety, free breakfasts in the morning (to cut down on food costs), and guest laundry facilities. These amenities are not too hard to find and really can help with controlling costs and making the traveling easier.

Another important way to keep expenses down is to keep track of them. Forcing yourself to write down every penny you spend will have you looking at purchases in a more cutthroat way. I recommend keeping a notebook in the car with either a stapler or a roll of scotch tape. Every time you spend money, make sure to get a receipt and then place it in the notebook. Give each day of the trip its own page and at the end of the day, tally up lodging, food, gas, and souvenir/sightseeing expenses. Another benefit of this system is a visual record of spending that the children can see. They will get into the cost-containment thing and cut down on the whining they're prone to in gift shops. After I instituted this system on my first trip alone with the kids they reserved their requests for items they really wanted and not for everything that happened to catch their eye.

Feeding the starving posse is always an important aspect of any trip. Usually full children are content children and content children don't complain as much. The first thing to consider is any dietary limitations. If you have allergies or food sensitivities, lay in a supply of non-perishable alternatives that you can store in the car and use if in a pinch. My family happens to be vegetarian, and let me tell you, my trip through Kansas was difficult. There wasn't much there that didn't have beef in it. I thought we were going to starve through that state.

It's helpful to have a cooler in the back of the car so that you can keep some fresh food on hand. It also helps to have a garbage bag in the car for all the wrappers and other accumulated junk that needs to be thrown out along the way. Every time you stop for gas, use it as an opportunity to clean out the car. Let the kids hop out, stretch their legs, dump trash, put things back into place, and rearrange the items they want at their fingertips.

🔺 Unfortunately eating in the car over a period of time causes food particles to accumulate. When we were traveling across the country, we stopped in Rocky Mountain National Park to sightsee. We got out of the car at a scenic overlook and when we turned around to get in the car, we found a marmot had climbed in. This little creature had smelled a buffet and was feasting on bits of food dropped by the kids. We had quite a time convincing it to get out. After that we were more careful about picking up dropped pieces of food.

When I went to get the car detailed after the trip, the guy cleaning it wanted to know what had happened in the car, as he said it was the dirtiest one he had ever cleaned! I was so embarrassed, but what could I say? I'm content in the knowledge that the trip was a grand success.

Entertainment

Entertainment will be mostly directed at times in the car with a lot of driving. Long hours trapped in the car with children can be fraying on anyone's nerves. There are things you can do to make it more bearable.

First, before you go on your trip, research some of the things you think you'll be doing along the way. For example, when I toured the East coast with the kids, I knew that we would be focusing on colonial America. I was able to find several books and a coloring book at a local bookstore that I knew the kids would like. Don't forget to take along some in schoolwork that you normally do at home that can be transported easily, like math worksheets or vocabulary books. Try to organize everything into a small case that can be kept up front in the passenger seat or in easy access of an older child while you're driving.

There's nothing wrong with adding to resources along the way. Make sure you look in gift stores, museum shops, and souvenir stands for educational resources that can extend the learning at the places you visit. Also, don't forget to ask at various places that you visit. Often times they have brochures or other materials that aren't put out for the public but they'll gladly share with you upon request. This is often a successful technique because the kids are excited about the attraction they've just seen and will be kept busy with them for a long time. Along these lines, it's imperative to have a system for organizing pens, crayons, paper, etc. that the children can easily reach. There are inexpensive organizers that can be purchased to hang over the seat in front of the kids and can be filled with everything they could want. This way you won't have to pull over and stop when supplies are needed to complete a project.

There is nothing wrong with a healthy supply of books for your trip, either. Unfortunately library books aren't usually available because of their due dates and the likelihood of them being lost along the way. So, mostly you are stuck buying books to read. At the end of the trip you will be left with many books that have already been read and that you probably don't have room for.

I've found a wonderful resource on the internet, found at www.PaperBackSwap.com. You can list your gently used books, both paperback and hardcover, and when they're requested, you send them off to that person. In return you get a credit with which you can turn around and request a book for yourself. This is a great way to get rid of books you don't want to keep and also obtain some for the next trip.

Audiobooks are much the same as books in that you don't want to lay out too much money for them. Look for long audiobooks that you can listen to over a period of days. Cracker Barrel restaurants, usually found along highways, have a program where you can buy one audiobook and then return it for a refund at the next restaurant you run into for a small charge. Some truck stops have also started to institute programs like this; just keep an eye out for them.

Many people now have DVD players in their cars. This can be a lifesaver, but it can be easily abused. It's helpful to decide at the beginning of the day how much you'll let the kids watch that day and then try to keep the viewing to the later hours of the day. This is helpful because on long days of driving, when tempers are highest and everyone is tired of being cooped up in the car, the DVD will take the children's mind off of their discomfort. Don't squander these precious times on mornings when everyone is fresh and happy. DVD time for the kids will let you listen to some adult selections of music or the news on the radio and stay connected with the outside world.

Journaling

This next topic is so important, it deserves its own section. It's so easy to get wrapped up in all the fun things you're doing and seeing on a trip that you forget to write them down. Memories fade after time and it would be a shame to lose some of the educational value gained on a trip because no one can remember it.

There are several different ways to journal depending on your interests and those of your children. For an artistically minded person, a sketchbook or photo journal could be fun. For those children that like to write, a more narrative style will probably suit them better. But regardless of the method chosen, a journal will continue to delight your children long after the trip is over.

> ♠ At the beginning of every trip, I get each child a three ring binder with some plastic protector pages. We also take a small container with scissors, tape, glue, stickers, and markers. For every day of the trip, or every significant stop we make, the kids would make a journal page. It's a great way to keep a record of everything you aww along the way. I take a digital camera with me and every few days, I go to a Wal-Mart or Target and take out the memory stick and go to an automated machine to print out pictures. I print several copies and give them to the children for their journal, and some I send to friends and family members, so they could keep up with our journey.

For the kids, the journal is an individual expression of their trip. You can also sneak in school work if you want. If you want to work on composition skills, have your child write a few sentences on each page about their impressions before pasting pictures or making illustrations.

I found that saving brochures and maps of attractions we had visited was also fun for the journals. The kids got really good at cutting these things up and using them to decorate their pages. These journals continue to delight the children year after year. Every couple of months, my daughter will pull her journals out and flip through them remembering her trips.

Laundry

Laundry is a subject we all wish would go away. However, if you go on a long trip, you won't be able to take enough clean clothes to last. Staying at hotels with guest laundry facilities makes it easier. Make sure you take a supply of detergent with you, as it's just too expensive to pay for the small cartons each time. Also, make sure you lay in a supply of quarters to operate the machines.

Before the trip, try as best you can to research the average temperatures of the areas you'll be visiting. This is not always foolproof, so make sure you add a jacket for unexpected cool weather and sunscreen for unexpected hot weather. First figure out how many days rotation of clothes you want. I usually take a four day rotation, so I am not doing laundry all the time. Then, consider buying new clothes that are all coordinated. I know this might seem expensive, but you buy clothes for kids anyway; just make your next shopping trip specific to your planned trip. This means you can mix and match so that everyone doesn't have to wear the same four outfits over and over again. Trust me, after six weeks on the road, you will crave some variety.

> ▲ I just finished a three month, 13,000-mile long road trip with my kids this summer. We primarily focused on the Lewis and Clark trail, but hit many other sites as well. We purchased a pass to the National Parks and visited as many as we could along the way. I stuck with the four day rotation of clothes but got so tired of the clothes we took on the trip, I gave

them all away when we got home. I couldn't stand to see those outfits anymore!

On this trip, we got stuck in the most unbelievable heat wave – temperatures of 104 degrees when we hit New Orleans. Nobody was having any fun melting in that weather, so we cut our trip short there and made up the time by spending a few extra days in Florida where we had access to a pool and the beach at a relative's house. Sure, we missed a few things that I had counted on in New Orleans, but we made up for it by doing a few extra things in Florida including a boat ride through some mangrove forests. We did a little short unit on ecosystems to tie in the new experience, and everyone had fun.

Some of these tips and tricks will work for you and others won't. Through trial and error, you'll come up with a system that will be comfortable for you and your family. But sometimes, the most carefully laid plans can go awry. These times can't be planned for in advance; it's best to just go with the flow.

Issues like car trouble, bad weather, and illness can interfere with the best laid plans. This is where flexibility comes in. If you're too rigid in your plans and expectations you'll have some disappointments. Keeping your options open when life interferes will give everyone on the trip a better outlook and may lead to some fun, unexpected surprises.

♦ On one of our cross country trips, my son developed an ear infection. As he got sicker, I realized that traveling across the Rockies would probably aggravate his ear, so we decided to stay east of the Rockies for a while until he healed. We holed up in a hotel in Eastern Colorado for a few days and then spent a few more days exploring the place once he felt better. This was totally unplanned, but we got to see more things than we had anticipated. It was a fun extra week on the trip. By the time we resumed out trip, my son's ear was on the road to recovery and we had an uneventful time on the rest of the trip.

If there's one thing that you really need to take advantage of with homeschooling, it's this ability to take off and experience the world. Your kids will never forget it. There's so much that can be taught just by the new experiences you will find yourself in.

The ability to learn the same subject with different modalities will cement subjects in your children's minds and extend the learning opportunities exponentially. Your kids will never forget what they see and experience. Also there will be many times you run across people and places you didn't anticipate that will add to the educational process. Traveling for educational purposes can be tiring, expensive, and even scary, but the rewards are enormous when you consider all that can be taught.

11

The Myth of "Me Time"

One of the funniest questions non-homeschoolers ask is something along the lines of "Where do you find time for yourself?" The question makes me laugh because it assumes that parents can't be fulfilled and happy while being with their own children all day – that the presence of children interferes with adults' ability to accomplish what they want as individuals. Along the same lines is the question of "How could you give up your career?" which gives the impression that the harder you train or the more money you could be making, the more difficult it is to dedicate oneself to one's children. Yet when I talk to homeschooling parents in my own circle, in discussion groups, and at conferences, few if any people talk about the freedom, money, or careers they've given up; rather, they discuss the many ways in which their family has benefited from their lifestyle change.

Ask ten different homeschooling parents how they stay happy and you'll find ten different answers. Much like the process of discovering what style of homeschooling is right for a particular family, finding how to fit into the homeschooling lifestyle as an individual person takes thought and experimentation. Do you need to have a designated "me time" every so often, work outside of the home, treat yourself to a special day doing something you love, or hire a mother's helper every so often to help out around the house? Only you can answer the question of how to not lose yourself in this endeavor.

Meeting your needs will take work at first and will not come naturally; after all we as parents are pre-programmed to ignore our own needs and focus on our children. The difference with homeschooling is that your needs affect your ability to be an effective teacher. Therefore taking care of yourself, whatever that entails, needs to be a priority in your homeschooling lifestyle.

The first step is, of course, identifying those individual needs that you have and figuring out how to fulfill them. American society sometimes makes this difficult, since modesty and self-deprecation are often prized social qualities, but there isn't much that feels better than finding out exactly what you want and planning to get it.

 HOMESCHOOLING HIGHLIGHT:

Don't feel bad about taking time for yourself. You are the other half of the homeschooling relationship and you have the right to be as fulfilled as your children.

After all, your homeschooling style should reflect some general principles that will be true for you as well as for your family, but these goals and traits will have your children in mind more than you. You need to make sure that you add goals that will help you maintain your standards and meet your personal needs.

Meeting those needs isn't as hard as it might seem. For some homeschooling parents, meeting their needs both financially and personally involves working outside the home. It could mean continuing with hobbies or volunteer work. Or it could just be as simple as getting time to read a favorite book or get your nails done. Whatever it is that will make you happy, make sure you do it; it will help you be a better homeschooling parent.

Employment

There is no need to automatically table the question of career and working if you homeschool. There will be some alteration of the work, but it's still possible. If giving up one income is going to cause financial strain or cause one parent to feel unfulfilled, start looking for creative answers. The decision whether to work or not is just as much one that needs to be made based on external factors, like money, as internal factors, such as fulfillment and satisfaction. Don't feel guilty if the decision comes down to what you as the parent wants to do – after all, you are the other equal half of the homeschooling relationship.

Many of these decisions will depend on the ages of the children involved and how much time they need you physically present. It's much easier to leave independent learning teens for outside employment than elementary aged children.

If financial concerns are at the top of your list, first start by looking at your financial situation carefully. How much money do you spend currently on things that would disappear with homeschooling? School expenses can add up, especially if you were sending your children to private school. Even public schools have their way of worming money out of you with uniform costs, fundraisers, and extra-curricular activities. Transportation and child-care expenses that you incur when working outside of the home should also be factored in to savings.

If both parents need to work, is there a way for one working spouse to work nights and weekends? This can stagger the working hours, allowing one parent to be home with the children all the time. Can one spouse work part-time, cutting down on the time away from the children and thereby still allowing a full-time homeschooling situation to exist? Are there family members willing to help out or other homeschooling parents who can co-op and teach when you're not available? Can you take your children to work with you and let them do their schoolwork alongside of you?

♠ I was a partner in a busy pediatric practice for many years before I started homeschooling. After I had started homeschooling, the thought never occurred to me to give up working, so I started to work nights after teaching my children during the days, a scenario that worked great for me for about four years.

When we moved out to California, I was unable to find work during nights and weekends, so I decided not to work exclusively for a while. That didn't last for more than two months as we needed the money, so I decided to look for other types of work and change careers. I saw a job advertised for an evening medical professor needed to teach nursing and pharmacy students at a local community college. I had never taught before, but the decision was easy; remember my mission statement?

By this time I was firmly entrenched as a homeschooler, and I decided taking a new job was not going to interfere with these ideals. I started out by taking the kids to the job interview with me. I was professional but also made the point to my prospective employer that my family was central in my life, and hey, I was a homeschooler with a husband who worked. I had to bring them with me because I had nowhere else to put them. I was very pleased when I got a phone call the next day saying I had the job and asking when could I start. In a way, it was to my advantage to include my children from the beginning, because on the occasions when I had to bring them with me to work when my husband was not available, it was not seen as an unusual occurrence.

I know some of these scenarios are not always feasible, but with a little creativity it's usually possible to work out a solution. There are of course some jobs that are easier to do when caring for children than others, but usually homeschooling can be accommodated in some way for any profession. One mom I know was a teacher at a local private school. She worked part-time and was able to bring her son with her to work. He would sit in the back of the classroom and work on his own work while she taught the class. Another mother I know who home-schools her four children was a birth coach. She had an arrangement with another homeschooling mother that whenever she got called (and as you can imagine, it was very last minute notice), she could drop off her children.

It's important for the parent doing the homeschooling not to feel like they have sacrificed everything in order to do this. If a change of career is a welcome thought then by all means, consider something more flexible, but don't give up a beloved profession just because you think it will be too difficult. Homeschooling is hard enough without adding resentment on top. Also, don't worry if work time interferes with school time. After all, that's a lesson too in showing children what it takes to be successful and support a family. Look at it from the educational point of view. Homeschooled children often get to see their parents working hard to provide for their family, and as a result are less likely to take things for granted.

Pursuing Your Interests

Another way to find fulfillment as a homeschooler (my favorite) is to get the kids to like what the parent likes. If there's a book you want to read, if appropriate, read it aloud to your children. If you love to cook, get your kids in the kitchen helping you. If you like to shop, take them along and give them jobs to do while you look around, like picking out the right sizes of clothes you indicate to them. If you like to play tennis, let them act as ball boys and girls. The possibilities are really endless once you embrace the spirit.

I also enjoy needlepoint and cross-stitch. For a while I thought it was an activity best relegated to times when the kids were asleep, but one day I thought, why in the world couldn't I teach my kids? So, when each was about five, I started to teach both my son and daughter, and now we're able to sit down together and do our needlework. My son loves to knit and has made a few scarves for himself, much to my husband's chagrin. (But let me tell you – it really helped his fine motor skills when I was trying to teach penmanship.) My daughter enjoys needlepoint and cross stitch and has completed several projects. Sure, it takes me a little longer to accomplish things, but it's so rewarding to see their excitement at accomplishing along side of me.

◢ One homeschooling mother I know loved to read and always had a hard time fitting it into her schedule, so she started a science fiction book club for adults. A couple of times a week all her children read or play quietly while she reads her "assigned readings." She gets to relax for a while and engage in an activity that she truly enjoys. Second, her children see her pursuing personal interests, apart from school or work. What better way to reinforce the message of life-long learning and at the same time get personal time than to model your work and interests to your children?

Another homeschooling mom I know of takes off her mommy hat at 8:30 every night. By then the kids have been fed, bathed, and readied for bed. All that remains is a little play time and off to bed. The kids love it as they feel they get to stay up a little later, while she revels in the ability to check email, make phone calls, or peruse a catalog at her leisure without being bothered by children's requests for help or to negotiate skirmishes between siblings. And she doesn't have to resort to the wee hours of the night to get these tasks accomplished.

Another friend has a set nap time every afternoon. When the children were younger, they slept, but as they aged, nap time was turned into quiet time. There were no rules, only quiet time in their rooms. Everyone got to pursue their own interests and take time to recharge themselves.

When You Need to Get Away

There are days when everybody is cranky and nothing is getting accomplished. It could be frustration with a difficult lesson, sibling rivalry, or just seasonal – too much rain, snow, or heat keeping everyone cooped up inside. Numerous circumstances can cause tempers to rise and it's okay to feel like you don't want to listen to your children complain about their lessons, chores, or each other anymore.

However, don't think that simply getting away as from the kids will make things better; everyone will still be cranky, just separately. Even if you get time away from them, trust me, they'll still be complaining about the exact same things they were complaining about before you left them. And while maybe you'll have a little more patience to deal with it after a refreshing break, that patience will wear thin very quickly and you'll be right back where you started.

The key to managing these times is to try to defuse the situations and work through them with everyone involved. Find things that are reserved for these special cranky days. My family has a day at the movies or at the beach when this happens. Sometimes we have just a pajama day and rent a whole stack of movies and do nothing. I figure, if we stayed home and tried to power through our lessons, someone is bound to kill somebody else, so why not have fun instead?

If everyone is really sick of each other, consider outings together that will give everyone some space and yet still allow for a shared experience. No one says in a movie theater everyone has to sit right next to each other or at a museum be looking at the same exhibit at the same time. Shared experiences with a little separation while doing them can be just the thing to soothe tempers and readjust feelings.

TIPS AND TRICKS TO USE WHEN
YOU WANT TO RUN AWAY

Backwards Day: Serve dinner for breakfast, and continue that way throughout the day. Remember to "get dressed" at night and "undress" in the morning. The kids will have so much fun trying to figure it all out they will forget to be cranky.

Video Game Day: Everyone plays and tries to finish all the levels on a

---

favorite game no matter how long it takes.

Really Long Board Game Day: You know how you groan when the kids bring out *Monopoly* or *Risk* because you never have time to finish them? Well, now is your chance – play to the bitter end.

Movie Day: Go to a movie theater and see several movies or rent a bunch and watch them one after another. Maybe watch a complete series – like all the *Star Wars* movies. You'll be surprised how much fun it is to compare the different episodes when watched in close succession. We started a James Bond movie marathon one day and have continued it sporadically. As we have worked our way through the movies, we're keeping track of things like body count, evil henchmen, etc. It's fun to see how things change given the social and political climate of the years they were made in.

Puppet Day: Everyone has to make a paper bag puppet and use them to talk the entire day. Try to make the puppets as different as possible from yourself.

Go On Strike: Declare a strike and let the kids fend for themselves. Lay on the couch and insist they do all the household chores. Or better yet, declare yourself the Queen of the house and to have them serve you all day.

Beach/Park/Theme Park Day: Go to whatever local resource you have available and let the kids run wild.

Lose the Guilt

A lot of parents will feel guilty about focusing so much on themselves, but parents need to help themselves first for the health of the whole family, not just the children. If parents are truly happy and satisfied, their kids will sense that – just as they sense when parents are unhappy.

This sensitivity makes unfulfilled parenting doubly dangerous, because often children, who are naturally self-centric, will see themselves as the cause of adults' unhappiness. Children naturally generalize and internalize their feelings and reactions to all aspects of their lives in a single mass because the mental mechanisms that enable compartmentalization don't develop until later in life; as a result, children tend to blame themselves when they sense that something is wrong, even if there's no obvious connection to themselves. Even mature teenagers have trouble seeing parental actions as a response to unrelated elements of their lives, like financial worries or marital stress.

In some ways, people who send their children to traditional schools do have an easier situation: They have scheduled time away from their children without extra expense or difficulty in which they can work on some of these issues in their own life. Even so, many of the mothers I met during my years of medical practice expressed frustration and almost resentment of their situation with regards to children and family life. I heard mothers say more than once that they couldn't wait for summer or vacation time to end so their kids could go back to school. This frustration was born out of the unfulfilled needs of the moms, subconsciously feeling that if it wasn't for their kids, they would be able to do all of their favorite things.

While homeschoolers don't have this same advantage of scheduled child-free time courtesy of the state, they can still get their needs met just by following a few easy strategies that just take a little thought and practice.

Knowing that their kids are around means that homeschooling parents need to have good support systems in place. You need to anticipate times when you might need help and make arrangements before they happen. These can be made with other homeschooling friends, family, or neighbors. Not only will you have to get help with the care for your children, but also with their schooling. The flexibility of homeschooling allows tremendous leeway and while sometimes taking a "vacation" from schooling is the best response to a crisis, there might be times when outside help will be necessary.

> ♠ A homeschooling friend of mine recently had an eye-opening experience where she needed a lot of support. Her husband collapsed one day at work from a brain aneurysm. He was in critical condition for several weeks but thank goodness was able to recover and was finally able to return home.
>
> Obviously, this family had a lot of stress and turmoil, and unfortunately had very little support from family nearby. It was heart-warming to see our homeschool support group spring into action and help out. We took turns watching her children and helping to continue their lessons.
>
> While this is a terrible situation for anyone to be in, if it wasn't for the support of the homeschooling network, things would have been a lot worse. In talking to this mom, she really felt that had she not had others to rely upon, she would have had to put her children back in traditional school. Her husband's recovery took almost a year and she didn't want to ignore teaching her children for that long.

Considering how you'll deal with situations before they arise will in and of itself help you navigate them more smoothly. This will enable you, when these life situations crop up, to deal with them quickly and not be fettered with unresolved personal feelings. Nothing leads to resentment faster than martyrdom. If you don't adequately address your needs, whatever they may be, and take the time to care for yourself, you'll start down that road to resentment.

Don't be shy about telling your family that you're figuring out how to meet your own needs. It's very easy for other family members to take for granted the parent who stays home and homeschools. After all, they are able to spend the day in the comfort of their own home, surrounded by sweet, smiling cherubic faces; what more could a homeschooling parent need?

The reality of doing mountains of laundry and washing dishes (because for some reason people seem to think these tasks are intimately associated with teaching your children) and constantly reminding your children to pick up their clothes and pay attention to your teaching are enough to make anyone beg for time away.

Letting your children in on this process is just another way that you can teach them a life lesson. Children don't need to know all the details about everything happening in the family and what they need to know will change as they grow and mature, but letting them in on some details will be just part of the great education you're giving them so they can be better, more capable adults.

Being vocal about your needs will set a good example for your children. They will learn not to subjugate their personal needs either later on in life, and it will also help them to recognize their own needs as people, hopefully heading off some of the issues that young adults face that can derail them from a successful future.

The final thought I have on the "me time" question involves role-modeling to your children. We are our children's heroes and they do look up to us, even though we swear they don't listen to a word we say. As such, when we are frustrated, tired, angry, or worn out, they will be watching and copying our behavior. A fellow homeschooling mom remarked to me one day that she found it so frustrating that all her bad qualities seemed to be magnified in her daughter. Well, they seem so because her daughter watches her and internalizes what she sees. I often used to complain to my husband about how the kids had a radar for my bad days, and choose to act just as heinous as they could when they found one. I considered it a cruel joke of the parenting gods until I thought about it for a while.

Children will soak up anything around them, good or bad. When you're in a bad mood, they will be too. When we say we need time away, or adult conversations, our children will simply respond in kind. All of a sudden you will wonder why they prefer the company of their friends over their family or shun you when they're in need. They're doing nothing more than parroting adult behavior. This is particularly problematic in homeschooling because it can impact the learning that should be taking place. So the next time you feel guilty about taking time for yourself to alleviate these frustrations, realize you're actually going to improve your homeschooling success.

Below I've listed some common complaints from homeschooling parents, including some I've used myself. They're natural; instead of feeling bad for not being perfectly pleased with everything, consider what you can do about their sources.

I need to get away from my children for a while.

Especially if you're homeschooling and parenting a challenging child, you might think this a lot. Thankfully, it's one of the easier problems to solve. In chapter 9 we talked about methods of learning that don't involve you directly, such as small group classes and sports teams. Just figure out what places you can use these enrichment classes for the maximum benefit for both you and your child.

One word of caution: It's tempting to drop the children off and spend the time doing errands, but that negates all the benefits of "me time". Errand lists always return; the time is better spent recharging. Forcing yourself to have some downtime will give you that calm time you desperately needed.

My spouse and I need more time together without the children around.

It's important for the health of a family to have spousal alone time. Interpersonal relationships take time and effort to maintain and the bond between parents is no different. The day-to-day activities of the primary homeschooling parent will be different from those of the primary income earner, and without time to talk with one another it's easy for spouses to lose track of what the other deals with. Deadlines, meetings, and workplace frustrations are wholly different stresses than those of cranky children, meal-time preparation, and the continuous work of teaching.

Making sure that you connect with your spouse takes work and attention. While it's tempting to arrange this time for night-time when the children are already in bed, make sure that this time is special for things you would not want to share with your children. The mundane communications, decision-making, and general sharing is easily done during the day. If the phone rings, ignore it. If a child asks for attention, give them a firm but agreeable no and then a time period when you'll be available. There's nothing wrong with assigning school work, chores, or play time during this time.

> ♠ When I first mentioned to a friend that my husband and I carved out Mommy and Daddy time and didn't let the kids intrude on us during this time, she was shocked and couldn't understand why we would want to take time away from our kids. I felt a little guilty until I reasoned that she sent her kids to school and really didn't see them all that much. When you spend all day with your children, fifteen minutes with your spouse is perfectly acceptable.

It's also very important for children to see their parents taking this time together. Let them know why you are doing it and what you talk about. The specialness of a committed relationship and the bonds that are implied make it all the more important for children to see the effort parents go to maintain it. What better way is there to ensure your children understand the work involved in a relationship than to show them on a daily basis?

I need more adult contact and adult conversation.

This common complaint can be dealt with pretty easily with the cooperation of other homeschooling parents, who probably also feel as you do.

> ♠ I personally found the solution to this one through a fellow homeschooling mom. I was out to lunch with her and all of our respective children one day when she rearranged the sitting arrangements to have all the kids at one end of the table and the two of us at the other end.

Initially, I had a lot of consternation about this as I usually positioned myself within an arm's reach of my children (in case the need to whack them came up at the table). Well, the arrangement worked fabulously. The adults were happy to be able to talk and the kids were happy knowing that we were not all over them for every little thing (as long as they met the general rules for decorum). The next time we met, we went a step further and got a separate adult table next to the kids table. This has been such a successful method that now, whenever a group of us goes out to eat, both the kids and adults expect and demand their "own" table.

On a day to day basis, whenever you feel you need more adult time, schedule a play date or go to park day. The kids are thrilled to have unstructured play time and the parents can sit around and talk and visit. The one group that will have trouble with this method is parents of toddlers. There's not much that will keep a toddler busy and occupied that is safe and allows the parents to put their attention elsewhere. Just be assuaged by the knowledge that this phase will pass.

Hopefully, I've addressed some of the barriers that parents perceive are in their way of full and complete enjoyment of immersing themselves in their children's life. The answers to these questions of how to get "me time" into your life might surprise you and the creative ways you find to solve them will serve to enrich not only your life, but your whole family as well.

PART 4:

Beyond Homeschooling

12

The Unenlightened

There are certain inevitabilities that come with homeschooling. You will forge a stronger bond with your children, you will adjust to being in control, you will realize that education is a life-long process that you only start your children off on, and at some point in your homeschooling journey you will run across people that do not approve of your educational choices or your resultant lifestyle. They can pop up anywhere, in social situations and even in your own family. Even supermarket cashiers will give you their opinion once they find out yours is a homeschooling family. These people will run the gamut from very vocal to quietly subversive, but you will still have to deal with them.

🔔 A perfect example of this occurred a few weeks ago during a committee meeting for one of the volunteer organizations I'm involved in. A perfectly fine meeting had been derailed by one of the other adults who obviously had something out for me. I was so upset that I zoned out a moment, but then something snapped my attention back real quick. I heard the words, "You homeschooling types…" and I knew with startling clarity what the problem was. It had nothing to do with my responsibilities or performance and had everything to do with what I represented, the lifestyle of homeschooling. This individual went on to complain that I shouldn't be in charge of setting outing times as "homeschooling types" never have to get up early for anything and that I shouldn't be involved in setting the calendar because I have no comprehension of a school calendar since I had no schedule. She was voicing all of her stereotypes about homeschoolers.

I refer to these people as the Unenlightened. They come from primarily two places: those that secretly envy homeschoolers, but don't have the confidence or will to homeschool their own children (the Wannabes) and those that actively disapprove of homeschooling (the Disapprovers).

The Wannabes are the most difficult group to deal with. These people are often recognized by the statement, "I would love to homeschool my children, but I just don't have the _____ (patience, time, willpower, know-how, etc.)." It would be nice to think everyone in this category could achieve the inner confidence and courage to undertake homeschooling, but realistically this is not going to happen. Their resentfulness of your lifestyle can color all your interactions with them. Their opinions are almost impossible to change because they arise from internal factors rooted within their persona, so you're left with their niggling envy, which translates into dislike that often doesn't ever get mentioned. Often if you confront them directly, they will deny any negative feelings and in truth might not even recognize they are there.

In contrast are the Disapprovers, who are more vocal and more overt in their feelings. They have no problems with just coming out and stating their disapproval of your choices. However, sometimes they can be easier to deal with as their feelings do not originate within themselves and their own situation, but rather in dogma and tradition. No matter how much you try to convince certain people or present them with concrete evidence, they will never understand homeschooling. They will stubbornly persist in their beliefs that traditional schooling is the only way to educate children. They will gloss over the plain facts of increasing dropout rates, graduating high school students that don't possess even rudimentary skills, and the rampant safety problems faced in public schools today. Many times these people will have a background or career in education and will be inculcated in the party line of our current educational model. Usually these people are very vocal about how homeschoolers are ruining their children and are quick to point out the benefits that brick and mortar institutions can provide. But be confident in the knowledge that these very people can often be homeschooling's strongest converts when they realize some of the educational philosophies they hold so dear are false. Their opinions tend to be based on external measures of success and research, so sometimes with enough evidence and time, they will change their minds.

♠ At a recent homeschooling conference I listened to the story of a mom who had run across a Disapprover. She was at swim lessons with her oldest child and she struck up a conversation with a mom sitting next to her. The other mother was very interested in homeschooling and was asking all of the usual questions about socialization, curriculum, etc. They were having a nice conversation when suddenly a third mother, who had been sitting behind them, got up and said in a loud voice, "I can't believe what I'm hearing. I'm a teacher and I can't sit here and listen to this drivel. Homeschooling is wrong and can only severely hurt the children involved. They will be stunted academically and socially." She stomped off, leaving the other two mothers staring after her with their mouths hanging open. This was obviously someone who was very vocal about her disapproval and very confident in her own decisions.

But regardless of where the Unenlightened party is coming from, you stand in their way, representing not just an educational choice, but a complete lifestyle that they disapprove of. While to some extent, dealing with the Unenlightened gets easier as you homeschool longer, it can still take some wind out of your sails. As you become a more seasoned homeschooler, you will rack up successes and become more confident in your choices, but even experienced homeschoolers can get discouraged in the face of continued criticisms.

Not feeling prepared to handle these situations can derail even successful homeschooling families. Doubt will creep into all the chinks of your armor as you feel the suffocating pressure to conform. Nevertheless, these aren't personal attacks, and there are some tactics that you can rely on to help you navigate these circumstances and emerge victorious. Which of these tactics you choose to use will depend on whom you're talking to and the situation in which you find yourself.

1. Honesty and Openness

Sometimes, people are just suspicious about choices that are different from the mainstream. They think homeschoolers might be closet abusers and that homeschooling is just a way to keep the kids out of the public eye. Homeschooling might appear to them as a sign of radical politics or religion. Honestly explaining the realities and reasons of homeschooling can put many people's worries to rest.

2. Ask for Time, Free of Judgments

This works very well when you know the Unenlightened party and see them often. Close friends and family who initially disapprove of the choice to homeschool can usually be swayed with time and attention. Explain your motivations and your goals. These people, antagonistic as they may seem, are usually motivated by love and concern for you and your children. Acknowledge that love and concern and ask for their support in the form of six months of watching your homeschooling experience without negative comments. Seeing how wonderfully children grow and flourish with time in a homeschooling environment is all the evidence you will need to provide.

3. Silence

The next coping strategy is simple silence. Often this is successful with people who just want to make sure that you've considered all the possibilities and are pretty comfortable with your choices once they have reassured themselves. Just listening and allowing these people to share their opinions can often defuse the situation.

4. Avoidance

Some people might consider this the wussy way out, but sometimes it's for the best. Some people won't listen to you no matter what. These people can be destructive to your self-esteem and motivation, especially if you're at a rough time in your homeschooling journey. Just being around them can bring you down and make you question your choices. When this is the case, the best strategy is to avoid these individuals all together.

5. Gentle Pressure

Gentle pressure might also be called "nagging" by some, though I like to think of it in a better light. Oftentimes you can just wear down the Unenlightened with repeated exposure and discussions about homeschooling. You can slip comments into conversations, point out instances of your successes, and generally wear your homeschooling lifestyle on your sleeve. Since homeschooling has such a large impact on your life, it isn't hard to talk about it all the time.

6. Come Out Firing

This strategy is the most fun, but it also takes the most guts. This strategy simply turns questions back on the askers. For example, when someone asks whether you're worried about socialization, the gutsy thing to respond would be something along the lines of, "Aren't you worried about your children being socialized into an atmosphere of drugs, school shootings, and popularity contests?" These types of questions tend to shut people up really fast.

I've seen this strategy employed with mixed results. Many times the asker is just stunned, as most people expect you to defend your choices and not turn the argument around. However, sometimes, people are offended and fire back or just stomp off. You need to have a thick skin and be able to brush off the reactions of others. This strategy is probably best with people you won't meet again!

6. Come Out Firing

All of these strategies can be successful, depending on your audience and what you feel capable of in the moment. Being able to defend homeschooling choices in the face of disapproval helps develop confidence. When we reach difficulties in our own homeschooling journey we can use these same arguments to ourselves.

As homeschoolers it's our responsibility to be advocates of homeschooling. We need to show the world that we are normal, mainstream people who are doing the best that we can for our children. When we meet the Unenlightened, it's a noble goal to feel like we can convert them and strive toward that end, but stay realistic – it isn't always possible.

13

Where Does Homeschooling End?
College and Beyond

There's always angst in homeschooling circles about preparing children for life beyond homeschooling. Any time you get two or more home-schooling parents together, I guarantee that at some point a discussion of life beyond will come up. College versus technical school, how to make a transcript, the importance of having a high school diploma; these are just some of the hot topics in homeschooling groups. People who have older children that have "graduated" from homeschooling are revered and venerated with the successful launch of their children out of their house. Those who have younger children are consumed by worry about this step and continually seek out advice and reinforce-ment from those that have gone before.

Many of the next steps after elementary and secondary education are easily accomplished by children in traditional school settings. Tra-ditional schools are set up to prepare children to take those next steps, and in fact measure their successes partially by the outcomes of the next steps. Because of this fact, traditonal schools are always helping children work toward these goals, publishing and arranging test dates, setting up counseling sessions, and even arranging job fairs. However, remember that while schools are very focused on the next step, they rarely help children beyond that.

In contrast, homeschoolers are more concerned with life-long education, and while they are concerned with the next steps, they are also looking forward and beyond just the next step. We also don't have a system in place to notify us of test dates, arrange testing locations, and procure a copy of the high school transcript.

So, how do we prepare our children for the next step while staying true to our homeschooling ideals? How do we make sure we continue the whole-life approach to education while preparing for applications and interviews? How do we not get carried away with assessments, measurements, and comparisons, when many of these next steps are based on the very concepts?

The answers are relatively easy, and just like everything else we have discussed, very individual. The difference in this aspect though is that your children will have to take a more active role than many other aspects of homeschooling. At this point, you can lead, suggest, and facilitate, but the actual desicions need to be made by your children; after all, it's the rest of their life they are preparing for.

It's important to think about "graduation" before it becomes imminent. While I don't advocate adjusting any of your homeschooling choices around admissions requirements or applications for apprenticeship, it does pay to be aware of what you'll be facing and be prepared. If you think your child will be attending college, you'll want to make sure what you teach can be molded into a competitve application. If your child wants to pursue a vocation, make sure you can put together a compelling story for an apprenticeship or internship. Think of yourself as a public relations manager for a corportation. You don't want to compromise your ideals or educational goals, but you can put a spin on your children's accomplishments to make them attractive and desirable to certain groups. For instance, if you've taught your child a comprehensive algebra course and your child is applying for a vocational school, you'll emphasize the importance of their teaching with regards to problem solving skills and real-life applications. The same algebra course could be presented as a rigorous building block for higher mathematics for a college-bound student.

 HOMESCHOOLING HIGHLIGHT

It pays to be informed. Anticipate what your child might want to do and start researching requirements early. Don't solely let this guide your teaching, but do keep it in mind.

In covering what happens after homeschooling, I will break it down into several different parts that will take you through the process of graduating your child from high school and then admissions into college or vocational school. There are also several related topics in this discussion that we will cover as well, such as work experience and volunteer work.

High School Diplomas and Transcripts

One of the first hurdles to overcome is that of a high school diploma. There are several ways to obtain a diploma, but first there's a question of whether your child needs a diploma at all.

Let's first tackle whether a high school diploma is necessary. For the most part, I would say the answer to that question is yes. But as always, there are a few exceptions to this rule. If your child is very young, and has been accepted into college early, then the necessity of a high school diploma is questionable. But even in this case, there could be a benefit to having a diploma.

In many instances, at some point in life, there will be a line on an application that asks where a high school diploma was received and in what year. These are usually applications for government jobs or other bureaucracies that focus on completeness and not necessarily sensible information. If a person has a college degree you would think the presence or absence of a high school diploma would be superfluous. However, sometimes it's easier not to argue the point and just be able to fill out an application to completion.

⚓ Just last year, my husband was going through a security clearance for work because of a new government contract his company had signed. On the initial form, he had to fill out his high school information and provide a copy of his high school diploma. This was the first time he had been asked for his diploma in all the years he had worked. And you can imagine that if he had left it blank, there would have been a lot of explaining to do.

Unbelievably in a coincidence, just after this episode, he was filling out an application to obtain his CPA license in a new state. It was simply a formality since he already had a CPA license in two other states, but on the form again he was asked for his high school information. This example shows how things can be important twenty years later that you could never have anticipated.

There are several different ways that homeschoolers can get a diploma. The first is to obtain a diploma from an accredited school. This option is only available for those students who have attended some sort of program through which an official diploma is available. There are several on-line programs that have diploma options available. Obtaining a diploma through one of these sources either means solely taking their courses or taking some of their courses and submitting some of your work with your child for their consideration for awarding credit.

Of course, using one of these options means that you will have to give up some measure of control in your homeschooling. Diplomas come from these institutions with requirements, and these requirements vary depending on the institution. Also, these requirements may or may not meet the goals you've established for educating your children. Don't feel like this is the only option for a diploma though.

There's no need to automatically make yourself beholden to another for accountability in the education of your children as you will have undermined the very premises that led you to homeschooling in the first place. But, on the other hand, if this fits well with your homeschooling philosophies and the goals you and your children have, by all means take advantage of it.

The next option is to create your own diploma. Just because you have taught your child at home does not mean that your diploma is not worthwhile or useful. The diploma that you generate from your homeschool program has as much credence as any diploma from any other traditional school.

 HOMESCHOOLING HIGHLIGHT

Always take the easy way out. If a diploma option is available at little extra charge, avail yourself of it, but don't twist yourself or your children around to meet the obligations if they do not work for you.

The first consideration is the name of your school. Just like the name of any school, you want your name to be professional. Make sure you use your school name on the paperwork you file with the state or school district or wherever you file for homeschooling. Then once you're ready, print out an offical certificate on card stock with your school name and your child's name with some fancy wording and voila, you've made a diploma. Alternatively, most homeschooling organizations have graduation ceremonies and will supply you with a formally printed diploma to your specifications should you choose to involve your child in the ceremony. The best road to choose is the one that your child and you mutually agree upon. But we're getting ahead of ourselves a little here. Before you can print out and award a diploma, you need to certify that your child has met the requirements for graduation and has a transcript to prove it, which means figuring out what the requirements are for graduation.

There are two categories of requirements to remember here. The first ones are those that you and your child have set forth in your homeschooling journey. These will vary from family to family and reflect the values of your homeschool scenario. The second set of requirements are those set forth by the state in which you live. The easiest way to determine these is to check with the local public school district and see what their requirements for graduation are. These tend to be somewhat similar state to state but there are some variations that you will need to watch out for. There are many requirements for health education, PE, and drivers education that often need to be met in addition to the typical math, science, and social studies credits.

Now, before you get all upset about how to meet these requirements, remember, be creative. Meeting these requirements is rarely difficult for homeschool children. Health education can be done through biology or anatomy. PE requirements can be met through competitive sports or even scouts with camping and hiking. The same can be said for even traditional requirements like foreign language. Sign language can be used to meet this requirement. Also, traditional classes can be met with credit from life-experiences as well. For social studies credit, it's perfectly okay to use travel as a credit. There is no right or wrong, only what you feel comfortable justifying to a college admissions board or other authority some day.

Once you determine the requirements for graduation, you need to morph what you have been teaching into those requirements. This is the step of creating a transcript, where you name the individual classes and assign credit to them. Usually it involves a brief description of the courses taught and books used. Obviously, English classes will involve reading and writing, but the exact content is up to you. History can be US, World, or even more detailed like focusing on the Roman Empire. Or it could even be living history through travel and museums. The individual courses and content will not be as compelling as the sum total of the story you're telling in the transcript.

HOMESCHOOLING HIGHLIGHT

Think of the high school transcript as a story you're telling to college admissions officers. It's the story of the homeschooling journey you and your child have been on. Make sure it's a compelling story.

Once you have made the transcript, you've to assign the grades. This can be the hardest part of your job. It goes against our nature to assign all A's to our own children. But don't feel bad - assign whatever grades you feel are appropriate. For the most part, they will be A's - after all when you work one on one with a child, you know when they master the material. But every once in a while, if you feel that your child has not mastered 100 percent of the material or has slacked a little on their work, you might assign a B or even lower. Assign grades honestly, from your heart, and be prepared to back them up, but do not be intimidated.

If you don't believe in grades, as many homeschoolers don't, then assign Pass/Fail or Satifactory/Unsatisfactory grades. There are many traditional schools that do this as well, so don't feel that your child's application will be the only one. There's no need to change or compromise your homeschooling ideals on the transcript. There is always a way to accomplish the necessary while staying true to your educational ideals.

If your child has elected to work or join the military, there might never even be a need to ever even show the transcript to anyone. I still think it is a good idea to make one, though; it's much easier to keep up with one as your child goes through the high school years than trying to invent one later from memory. Also, for those children who are applying to college, and vocational schools, it's also a good idea to include a letter with their applications from you the "homeschooling parent" that details your homeschooling philosophy and styles. This will serve to give your transcript more relevance to those who review it.

Many colleges and universities use the common application form for students. There is a homeschool supplement that is woefully inadequate for telling your homeschool story. It consists of two pages with not much space available for explantions. So, even if you use this supplement, I would still recommend attaching a letter as detailed above. It doesn't need to be long and it doesn't need to divulge personal information that you don't feel comfortable revealing. For instance, if you started homeschooling your child because of behavioral problems in elementary school, there's no need to share that information. The admissions committee will be more interested in your methods of homeschooling and the means by which you achieved it. Appendix D contains a sample letter. Remember in this letter to toot your child's horn for them. If your child has accomplished extraordinary things, be sure to include them. Do not exaggerate, but make sure the admissions committee has a chance to learn about the deeds. Believe me, if you don't, no one will toot their horn for them.

TEMPLATE FOR A HOMESCHOOLING SUPPLEMENTAL LETTER

Introduction: State your reason for writing the letter with a brief introduction of what your child is applying for. Admissions committees read thousands of applications and you need to constantly remind them what this is for.

Academic background: Succinctly summarize your child's academic background. There's no need to hide any part of it. If your child has not ever been in traditional school, then state that. If they have been in and out of school, that is okay too. Just give a justification for whatever their background is, however, do not state any negatives. If you decided to homeschool for behavior reasons, keep that to yourself. You can just state that traditional classrooms did not offer your child the complete

---

education they needed.

Homeschooling philosophy: A paragraph or two can be included to delineate your homeschooling style and methods. Any style can be included here. Even if you're an unschooler applying to a university, you will emphasize the self-directional method of your child's education. Just make sure to focus on the aspects of the education your child received from you that will impress the particular institution to which they are applying to.

Accomplishments that are applicable: In this I mean the type of things the institution will want to see. If it's a rigorous university, you'll want to emphasize academic accomplishments. If it's vocational school, you'll want to emphasize practical experience. Do not feel that these need be only those accomplishments that are externally validated. There are plenty of things that are impressive even if they're not a part of a competition or didn't have a grade assigned to them.

Accomplishments that are not directly applicable: Here is a homeschoolers chance to shine. Here will be the meat of the letter in which you really focus on how great your child is and all of the things they have accomplished that traditionally schooled kids could not hope to accomplish. This will include work experience, scouting, other clubs, and any other extracurricular activities.

Any extras: If you haven't already mentioned these, make sure you include all the little extras, like sports, hobbies, and interests. Make sure also to play upon the personality strengths of your child. One or two sentences describing them will be helpful in completing the story you're telling about your child.

Closing: Pretty self-explanatory, but a last chance for a good impression to the admissions committee to remind them to look at the rest of the application.

Work and Volunteer Experience

Because of the freedom in their schedules, many homeschoolers have work and/or volunteer experience. This can be very important for future success both for higher education and for vocational work.

If your child is thinking of pursuing a vocational career, experience in the field can make all the difference in being accepted into an internship or vocational school. People are going to be more likely to take a chance on a child who has demonstrated skills and abilities versus an unknown quantity. If your child is going to pursue education at a university, previous work experience will show the admissions team that your child has the ability to be accountable and responsible. These qualities are prized by colleges who many times worry about children making the leap from secondary school, where everything is laid out and scheduled, to a college setting where self-motivation and personal responsibility are the tools for success.

It can be hard to find employment for your child, especially if they're young. Many establishments are reluctant to offer employment to children under the age of sixteen. Don't fret about this; volunteer work is a great way to get your foot in the door. Where employment is not an option, volunteers are often welcomed. Many government or charitable organizations are not able to offer employment and can only offer volunteering. This is not an important distinction. For the purposes of learning and experience, volunteer work is just as important as paid work, assuming you can prove that there was a level of responsibility and self-direction in the work accomplished.

As soon as your child secures a position, start thinking about a letter of recommendation. It could be from a direct supervisor or a coworker, but be sure it's someone with direct knowledge of the work your child is doing and who can point to specifics. Specific knowledge is better than the most glowing recommendation written in generic terms.

Setting Yourself Apart

One of the most important things a child can do in their high-school years is to try to set themselves apart from others in a significant way. If your child has a talent for competitive sports, a musical instrument, or other artistic pursuit, this will be an easy task. If your child has worked full-time, had a hobby, or attained their Eagle Scout rank from Boy Scouts or their Gold Award from Girl Scouts, it's also easy. But if this does not describe your child, do not worry yet. There's still time.

The sad fact is that when you apply for something desirable, whether it's university admission or a prized slot at a vocational school, or a scholarship, there will always be several other qualified candidates competing for the same slot. Given this fact, you see why it's so important to have something that your child can point to that will set them apart from others.

Start thinking about this early on in high school and allow your child to be a part of this process. Actually, they will be driving this whole process much more than you will be. As parents, older and wiser, we can point out these facts to our children, but they ultimately have to accomplish them. If your child has no ideas, then brainstorm with them. Start with their passions and hobbies. Are there clubs they can join and get involved in? Are there jobs or volunteer opportunities they would like to get involved in? Are there any family members or friends who can help out and suggest ideas or provide opportunities? Below I have put together a short list of ideas to get the ball rolling, so to speak. Once your child figures out the goal here, you will be surprised at how enthusiastic they become.

IDEAS ON EXTRACURRICULAR ACTIVITIES

Volunteering at the public library: There are usually a myriad of jobs to do at the library, from leading a story time to reshelving books, that are suitable for even very young teens.

Writing an article for a local newspaper or publication: Most communities have small publications quarterly or monthly that carry local articles. If your child can get one published, they can call themselves "a published writer".

Starting a business: Whether it is dog-walking, pet-sitting, baby-sitting, or yard care - just printing up a few fliers and business cards takes it to another level.

Starting a blog: This shows a lot of technical skill and savvy. One caution though, make sure it is something your child is proud of and would want an admissions committee to see some day.

Photography: If your child has access to a camera, have them take pictures and submit them to various publications. Just like writing an article for a local paper, photos can get published as well.

Getting a Future Direction

One of the most important things homeschooling parents can give their children is a future direction. This doesn't have to be set in stone; it can and should change with time, but the fact that it was thought about is the key point. It's easy to get caught up in the day-to-day humdrum of homeschooling and forget everything else. We have to worry about deadlines for testing, applications, recommendations, and a myriad of other things that traditional schools outsource to employees who are not taxed with education. We have to do it all and it can seem overwhelming educating. But just because it's overwhelming doesn't mean that we can forget and ignore it.

> ♠ I was talking to a fellow homeschooling mom a while ago about life after homeschooling. She related a story to me about a young woman she had met at a park one day. The young woman was a nanny to a wealthy family. She had been homeschooled her entire life and had graduated from high school several years earlier. She didn't know what she wanted to do, so she had drifted around for a few years until getting this job. She was happy enough, and was thoroughly happy with her homeschooling past, but her one complaint was that she didn't have any direction when her high school years were done. She said her mom had been so focused on teaching her in the moment that her future had never been discussed.
>
> This young lady felt she had been left without a clear plan and had drifted because of it. My friend and I discussed this point, agreeing that it is all too easy to get caught up in the moment and forget about the future.

Unfortunately, as much as we would like to keep our children by our side forever, they will grow up and will have their own lives. We need to prepare them as best as we can for the next steps in life. By the very nature of homeschooling, they will be better prepared than their traditonally schooled counterparts, if only by the fact that homeschooling teaches children how to acccomplish the daily tasks of life. Our children will understand how to negotiate obstacles that others have never even thought about, and have a degree of confidence and assurity with life's big picture. However, the future will not be obstacle free. Insulating our children from testing, comparisons, and meaningless beaurocratic red tape, while positive and worthwhile for the sake of education, will make these next steps of future navigation to seem a little harder. Looking ahead and planning for the future will allow smooth sailing through the confusing rough seas of the future.

14

The Big Picture

It's natural for you to want to share your successes and become a good-will ambassador for homeschooling once you're successful in your own homeschooling journey. There are opportunities to make a difference locally as well as in the wider world in terms of social, economic, and political impact.

Reaching out to others keeps our own lives in perspective and allows us, as homeschooling families, to continue to grow as we experience new ideas and philosophies. There's no better way to ensure that our children don't grow up self-centric than to get out into the wider world, promoting our cause while we learn from others.

Don't kid yourself that the skills you've learned as a homeschooling parent aren't valuable. The skills we acquire as homeschooling parents can be used in many ways. We can and should be leaders in organizations such as the Boy Scouts, Girl Scouts, Junior Achievement, athletic teams, etc. We should not limit our exposure to only groups of home-schooled kids, but be open to mentoring kids from traditional school situations as well. After all, we have more experience with teaching and problem solving with children than most other people. We are more aware of teaching styles and learning environments. The skills that helped us be successful homeschooling parents will translate beautifully into mentoring and leading other children as well.

Advocating Homeschooling

As homeschoolers, the logical place to start is advocating for educational freedom. In your own community, simply being visible and approachable is one of the most important ways we as homeschoolers can begin to change stereotypes and misconceptions about us. There's no need to feel like you should stay in the house during traditional school hours if that doesn't fit your needs. Unfortunately, there are still a few places in America where there are daytime curfews for children of traditional school ages. While homeschooling is typically regulated at the state level, I urge you to check your local government for any rules like daytime curfews that could affect your homeschooling lifestyle.

Make sure you get out on field trips and road trips. Don't hide the fact that you're homeschooling. While it's easy to not engage others when they don't know that you're homeschooling, like when you're at the grocery store and the clerk says, "Oh, your kids must be out of school today," I encourage you let them know you homeschool and what a great experience it is.

Another way to be visible and also to advocate for homeschooling is to join a local homeschooling group for both receiving and providing support to other homeschoolers. Not only is it a great resource for yourself, but it's a supportive medium in which to start speaking up and become comfortable with defending your educational choices.

Many metropolitan areas have homeschooling groups that are active in their communities. Simply googling homeschooling in your state is a great way to start connecting. Most state homeschooling groups have a listing of local groups. Also, check out some of the better known homeschooling websites, such as www.homeschool.com. Churches and community centers often have or know of homeschool groups, so don't forget to check with them.

These groups are often longstanding, usually having been formed years ago when homeschooling was not as prevalent or not even legal in all states. They are typically run informally with a couple of organizers who moderate email loops and publish calendars of get-togethers. Other than these common features, they can be very diverse. One group I was involved in was solely formed for the purpose of play groups and park days. Another group I was involved with had park days, but its focus was on co-op groups for teaching classes. And yet another one I have been involved with had support group meetings in the evening once a month where guest speakers were invited in to talk. Have an open mind as you investigate support groups - just like homeschooling, there really isn't one recipe.

If there isn't a local group easily accessible to you, consider starting one. Many times there are people out there who want to network but don't know how to get started. Finding other homeschoolers can be difficult, but here are a few ideas. Find an active homeschooling group that is near to you and send out an email stating you want to start a group in your area. You will often get a great response from people that know of homeschoolers nearer to you, or who live near you already but were using the resources of this other group because there wasn't one locally. Also check with the children's librarian at your local library to see if they know of any homeschoolers. The library is one place all homeschoolers come to eventually. Usually if the librarian doesn't know of any homeschoolers, they will let you post a notice to start a group.

Beyond your community, I strongly encourage you to support homeschooling at the state level. This can be done in several ways, most notably by supporting one of your state homeschooling organizations. Appendix C contains a list of some homeschooling organizations. Every state has at least one and oftentimes a number of large homeschooling organizations that operate to organize homeschooling on a larger scale. It's vital to join these and become involved. Again, not only are they wonderful places to meet people and gain ideas and support, they also function as watchdogs at the state level to inform you of any legislative or judicial problems that could have an impact on you as a homeschooler.

Also at the state level it's important for you yourself to keep abreast of issues that can affect homeschoolers. Usually state homeschooling organizations will watch these closely, but it pays to be informed. Make sure you know who your representatives are and contact them when issues arise that could impact educational freedom. The only feedback they get to decide these issues comes from their constituents, so make sure they know homeschoolers are living in their districts.

Despite the gains homeschooling has made over the past twenty-five years, we still need to be extremely vigilant on this level. The modern homeschooling movement really began in the 1970s, and by the mid-1980s there were an estimated 50,000 homeschooled students in the United States. However, homeschooling only became legal in all fifty states in 1993. Moreover, despite U.S. Supreme Court cases that have repeatedly supported a parent's right to homeschool, each state determines the amount of oversight or relative degree of freedom that we enjoy. This can vary from California's progressive homeschooling environment that only requires the family to annually register as a private school or Michigan's progressive laws where no registration or oversight is required to other states with extremely burdensome requirements such as those of New York, which has a nearly 3,000 word, 8-page list of regulations that includes getting annual approval on your curriculum from the local school district, listing required courses in your curriculum, maintaining attendance records in accordance with the public school policies, submitting quarterly reports to the school district, and taking an annual achievement test or completing an alternative annual assessment.

With our educational freedom being continually challenged, from school districts that tell families that homeschooling is illegal or that they must comply with rules that don't exist, to teachers' unions challenging the legality of homeschooling, we all must take responsibility to not only defend the hard-won freedoms that others have earned for us, but to also fight against more regulation and argue for more academic freedom.

🔺 In 2008 there was a very concerning challenge to the rights of parents to homeschool their children in California. A child welfare case was brought against a family who had homeschooled all five of their children, the older three being grown and out of the home at the time of the alleged abuses. The Los Angeles County Department of Children and Family Services asked that the two younger children who remained at home be enrolled in a traditional school setting so that their welfare could be monitored.

What was at issue in this case was not the quality of education these children were receiving but the fact that a parent was administering it instead of an unbiased third party. The lawyers wanted another set of eyes on these children, and most expediently chose a school. I would have hated to be the public school official tasked in this matter!

This case ended up by being appealed to the California Court of Appeals. A three-judge panel reviewed the case and then decided to make this a referendum on homeschooling, handing down a decision that parents do not have a constitutional right in the State of California to determine their children's education and deemed that no form of homeschooling was legal in the state. Education was meant in their eyes to be taught by credentialed teachers in a brick and mortar edifice. Unfortunately this ruling was not limited to the family involved in the case. Rather, the justices in this ruling used this case as a platform to declare that homeschooling of any type in California was illegal.

The justices wrote in their decision, "We agree…the educational program of the State of California was designed to promote the general welfare of all the people and was not designed to accommodate the personal ideas of any individual in the field of education." They went on to state in their decision that, "A primary purpose of the educational system is to train school children in good citizenship, patriotism and loyalty to the state and the nation as a means of protecting the public welfare."

Not surprisingly the ruling was applauded by a director for the state's largest teachers union. "We're happy," said Lloyd Porter, who is on the California Teachers Association board of directors. "We always think students should be taught by credentialed teachers, no matter what the setting." To understand how absurd this is, neither public nor private schools in California are required to hire only credentialed teachers. Moreover, much of what teachers learn in college and as part of becoming a credentialed teacher – from English as a second language to classroom management, multicultural appreciation, teaching students with disabilities, health education (recognizing and reporting abuse, alcohol, and drugs) and budgets and funding – has nothing to do with core education.

The repercussions of this ruling were unimaginable. All of the California homeschoolers were in state of panic, our conversations spanned the gamut from "going underground" and moving out of state to protesting and mounting a legal challenge.

An appeal was filed and the full Court of Appeals heard the case and vacated the earlier decision, ruling that homeschooling was legal in California. However, the case showed those of us who had become complacent with the freedoms we enjoyed just how delicate they were and how they still at any moment could be reversed.

Obviously, it's important to be aware of what's happening around you in the legal arena with homeschooling. The better informed you are, the better able to handle the challenges that might come along.

Above the state level, there are national organizations that support homeschooling as well. HSLDA (Home School Legal Defense Association) is one of the better known organizations that operates to defend freedom in educational choices and serves as legal counsel to its members who find themselves in legal battles over their educational choices for their children.

All of these organizations, from local to national and everything in between, help to promote homeschooling and its rights. It's important to be involved so that you can be aware of what is going on in the homeschooling community, obtain support and networking specifically for homeschoolers, and show your children the importance of advocating for the freedoms we're all benefitting from.

Advocating For All Children

As homeschoolers, we put the well-being of our children at the forefront of our lives. This gives the homeschooling parent a unique place in discussion about children and their needs in general. We have a lot to offer society and we shouldn't shrink from doing so. There's no need to hide the fact we're homeschooling or to adopt an attitude of elitism.

Advocating for all children means not just focusing on home-schooled children, but those in traditional school as well. We have a lot to add on issues of general child welfare and education in particular, no matter where it takes place, whether in the home or in a traditional school. We can also add to discussions in the political arena about child care, workplace situations, and children's rights.

The court case in California I previously mentioned was more than just a blow to the homeschooling community; it was a blow to parents everywhere. Parents are being told that they don't possess the ability to decide what is best for their own children. This extends far beyond education into other parenting rights. If we're not competent to decide how to educate our children, what are we allowed to decide?

Let's get back to education and take the state of public schools today as a start. Every child has the right to be educated, and we have a public school system in America that, for better or worse, tries to do just that. Even in rural areas, there's access to schools. We spend tax dollars bussing children to and from these institutions, providing food for those children that need it, and teachers to teach them. So why are we as a country upset with the state of the educational system?

Well, we have violence and drug problems in schools. There are problems with crumbling physical structures and unqualified teachers. We have rising drop-out rates and children who are almost illiterate at graduation. As reported in the 2008 National Report Card, our on-time high school graduation rate has decreased for all racial and ethnic groups over the past two decades. As of 2009, it was seventy-seven percent, the lowest level in three decades. As a result, the United

States is now ranked fifteenth out of twenty-nine countries based on the percent of adults who have completed college.

These are the very real problems that have driven many parents to homeschool their children. The quality of what's being provided and the ideal we as a society are striving for are worlds apart. However, just because we've chosen to remove our children from the traditional education system doesn't mean that we're not interested in improving it. We can and should lobby for better physical structures, pay raises for teachers, and an end to using standardized testing for funding decisions.

Homeschoolers are often criticized for withdrawing our children from the educational system. The argument is often made that when you withdraw the best students with the most involved parents, the whole system suffers. This argument is also being made increasingly today with respect to parents choosing private schools for their children instead of local public schools. While some may agree there's merit to this argument, consider that homeschoolers are allowing the public schools and governments to spend more tax dollars and resources educating others instead of spending it on our kids. We are still paying taxes to support public schools and in many instances taking nothing in return. The reality is that no parent is knowingly going to leave their child in a sub-par environment when there are better alternatives. We all want to be altruistic and selfless, but we don't want to sacrifice our children or their future for some ethereal claims.

But the fact that we are still tax-payers gives us the right to speak about issues that affect all children. The louder we speak out about children's issues, the more attention they will grab and also bring attention to homeschooling. The reality is that many of us will have children in and out of traditional schools at some point in childhood and we should try to make them as good as possible.

In this recent court case in California, there was a huge outcry and the media coverage went around the globe, from articles in USA Today and Time to news stories on CNN, NPR, and WorldNetDaily. I can assure you it was the main topic of conversation on homeschooling email loops. Most parents were eager to help and were asking what they could do. Many were clamoring to write or speak to their governmental representatives at both the local and state level to protest this ruling, but in the homeschooling community as a whole there was a reluctance to look for a legislative resolution for fear that it could result in additional oversight or regulations that would limit our homeschooling freedoms.

When the situation in California arose, I started to become concerned that the discussion about the homeschooling issue seemed to be dividing along party lines. Several times in the media, as this case garnered attention, homeschooling was touted as the sole purview of special interest groups, such as those who chose to homeschool for religious reasons or because of a child with special needs. This type of division is harmful for homeschoolers everywhere. Regardless of the reasons behind our homeschooling, we are all working towards a better education and lifestyle for our children and family. We're a varied and diverse group that mirrors the diversity in our society and we all have the same goal of preserving educational freedom so that we as parents can be the driving force in our children's life – not someone else.

So, as a liberal, tree-hugging, card-carrying Democrat, I wasn't about to let that happen. (I also got real excited about the educational opportunities this whole episode uncovered.) I started calling Democratic assembly members and senators and found there was little knowledge about homeschooling in general. I got the general feeling among democratic lawmakers that they did not feel homeschoolers were a part of their constituency. I could not let this opportunity pass me by.

I started making appointments to see some of these lawmakers. I wrote letters, gathered statistics, and put together folders of information to take to these people to help educate them. After driving through the interminable Central Valley in California, passing endless miles of farms, the children and I spent three days in Sacramento at our expense visiting legislative members and lobbying for support for homeschoolers. I even snagged an appointment with the chief of staff for the Speaker of the House. (How I managed that, I will never know.)

This was a wonderful experience, not only from the educational perspective of my children, but also I hope for opening people's eyes to the fact that homeschoolers are successful, normal-functioning families that contribute to society and the greater good. We are alive and well and exist in every ethnic and religious group, and we are very successful at raising and educating our children.

Not only should homeschoolers focus on child advocacy as a whole, I believe we have a lot to offer the educational system as well. Many of us have had children in and out of school during the course of our homeschooling years. We can and should speak about issues in a classroom. Even those of us who have never sent our children to school can speak to classroom issues because we are actively engaged in teaching. We can advocate for more school choice, better AP classes, establishing more neighborhood schools, and improving our schools' physical infrastructure, air quality, and safety. Even though our children may not be directly affected by these items, improving the overall educational system in America will benefit all of society and even our children someday. It would be wonderful to think they could avoid some of the societal problems we deal with now if we were able to fix them. Better use of our resources would result in more resources being available for environmental, medical, and other needs the government is facing. We don't want others following in our footsteps ten or fifteen years from now to be entangled in the same bureaucratic morass of regulations that fail to deliver a quality education in our public schools today.

Homeschooling and other non-traditional educational choices continue gaining in popularity, and homeschooling has definitely shown that it provides our children with a superior education. As homeschooling parents, we need to make sure these opportunities are available for everyone. Moreover, we should pass along the knowledge and experience that we've learned in our educational journeys so that others can benefit. Homeschooling definitely affects those of us who practice it, but wouldn't it be wonderful if the benefits could trickle down to all children?

FINAL THOUGHTS

Homeschooling is all about discovering what your children need and then setting about providing it for them. It is also a journey of self-discovery for you "the parent" to challenge your own assumptions and grow with your children. A successful homeschool family looks for solutions within the family unit and doesn't ascribe to outsourcing them to others without careful consideration.

Homeschooling becomes a natural outgrowth of the way your family life is organized. Whereas traditionally schooled children have their education looked at as simply a part of their life that happens 180 days a year, homeschooled children have their education wound into the very fabric of their life. Education becomes fun, interactive, and part of life, not something to be rushed through and finished with. Your homeschooling journey may end with graduation or matriculation back into traditional school, but you will find that homeschooling really never goes away. It is a way of living and looking at the world that will be with you and your children forever.

Appendices

Appendix A

Homeschooling Styles and Resources

This is by no means meant to be a complete list of homeschooling styles. I just wanted to highlight some of the more common styles and list a few resources for parents to start with. Just knowing where to start can be a helpful tool when beginning your homeschool journey.

Unschooling

Unschooling is basically child-led education. An excellent place to start investigating it is by reading any of John Holt's books. As well, this can be supplemented with any works by Pat Farenga, an educator who worked closely alongside John Holt and has continued his work by bringing his message out to many homeschoolers. And as with many other things, simply googling unschooling will bring a myriad of hits on the subject.

Lapbooking

This is a hands-on approach to unit studies for those children that are more tactile learners. As a child learns about a subject, they make a mini-book about it and then collect the mini-books together into a larger "lapbook" or folder. Just googling lapbooking will lead to many resources on several different sites as well as a yahoo group dedicated to homeschoolers that teach through lapbooking. Hands of a Child *(www.handsofachild.com)* is a wonderful website that sells lapbook packs already prepared for your use. They cover all ages and a wide variety of subjects. Once a quarter they also give away a free lapbook project that anyone can download.

Charlotte Mason

Charlotte Mason was an educator in Britain in the nineteenth century that popularized a curriculum based on instruction at home by parents with nature journals, living books, copy work, and narration. I am doing a disservice by trying to sum up her educational philosophy this quickly. You can easily read her books yourself or purchase a modern abridged version.

Several websites exist that are excellent tools to explain the Charlotte Mason method and I encourage you to use them. Even if after research, you decide to use another homeschooling method, they have wonderful lists of books to add to your homeschooling curriculum. I am sure there are other resources, but these are a good starting point.

1. *www.amblesideonline.com*
2. *www.simplycharlottemason.com*
3. *www.charlottemason.com*

Classical Education

Classical Education is a specific way of looking at education from the developmental point of a child. It divides the school years into three distinct areas: a grammar stage, the logic stage, and the rhetoric stage. These roughly correspond to a child's developmental capacity for knowledge. Very young children enjoy learning by repetition. They will soak up new material and are busy storing it away. By the age of ten or so, they start to ask questions and want some connections to be formed among all the facts they soaked up as young children. Then by high school age, children are ready to start making predictions and analysis of information with a degree of abstract thinking. They are capable of taking in information and then giving an analysis and an opinion, hence the rhetoric stage. There are many excellent resources for information on Classical Education but the best is *The Well-Trained Mind* by Susan Wise Bauer. It is a comprehensive resource of materials and curriculum as well as the philosophy behind certain choices. She has also published a number of companion texts for teaching literature, grammar, and history that are marvelous. I have also found the website *www.classical-homeschooling.org* to have many good resources listed as well.

Appendix B

Ideas for Homeschooling Co-op Classes

Bible Study
This can take any form that you want. There are a variety of resources available from workbooks to study aids. A fun suggestion would be to get a copy of the Bible on CD and listen to a part of it with each group meeting. You could study the geography of the Bible, ancient empires, ancient languages, and on and on.

Comparative Religions Study Group
A group of diverse students would enjoy this topic. A great resource is the Usborne book *World Religions*. I have heard of groups like this celebrating holidays according to other customs and even memorizing prayers from each different religion studied. If you live in a big enough metropolitan area, a field trip to a worship center for each of the religions studied would be fun.

Personal Finances
While this is suitable for any age, pre-teens could really have a great time with this. You could encourage them to make budgets for the entire family and try to balance the expenses. Even teaching mundane tasks like balancing a checkbook and using ATM's could be covered. One homeschooling mom I know used a conference room at a local bank to teach this class and had people from the bank in as guest speakers when appropriate.

Investment Club
This can be fun for older children. Give them a specified amount of hypothetical money to invest and see what they can do. You can use this as a platform for teaching about investments, different types of investing and accounts, and the tax implications of such. There is avail-

able over the web, a site that will track this for your students. *(www.
investopedia.com)*

Sewing
This can take many forms, from learning to use a sewing machine, to
hand sewing buttons, to learning embroidery techniques. My daughter
was privileged to learn from a mother who was very gifted in sewing.
The class was so fun it inspired me to learn how to embroider as well.

Quilting
When you find a parent who knows how to quilt, hang on to them. My
girl scout troop made several quilts for homeless mothers and had a
ball doing it. We scheduled several classes just for the girls to work on
their squares and then had a mom come and tie it together at a meeting. It was great watching the process (I know nothing about quilting)
and a class was spun off just on quilting from that.

Art
Many times you can find a local artist or even a homeschooling mother
that is talented and creative enough to start a class. Don't limit yourself
to just painting. There can be classes on sculpture, pottery, photography, drawing and illustrating, and the performing arts. One homeschooling group I was in was lucky enough to have a dad that had his
own business in lighting and props for performing arts centers. He and
his wife started a class in the performing arts, culminating in a play that
was professional in the extreme.

Cooking
This can be done by a professional, but if you do not have one available, don't fret. Every mother has a signature dish; just rotate teachers
and the kids will learn many different techniques and recipes.

Home Repairs
A most practical suggestion for any child to learn. All it takes is a handy

mom or dad to show children how to fix a leaky faucet, change light bulbs, replace screening, and use simple tools.

Hiking Group
For those who are outdoorsy, a hiking group or even a camping group could be a lot of fun. All it takes is someone with knowledge of the area and safety techniques. I have even heard of peak-bagger groups that go out every weekend and climb local mountains.

Roots and Shoots
This is a group started by Jane Goodall for educating children in conservation and environmental issues. Anyone can start a group; just contact their website and they will send you the necessary information.

Entrepreneurship
If you have motivated children with a bent towards business, getting them together can be very powerful. They can brainstorm ideas and then start to carry them out, learning about business practices in the meantime.

American Girl History Group
Obviously geared towards girls, the historical dolls have a wealth of information available including study guides. I started one of these for my daughter and was surprised at how informative it was. We learned geography, history, cooking, and literature, all based upon the historical dolls.

Sports
Pick your sport and get some kids together who enjoy it. There is no limit to this topic. I heard of a homeschooling rock climbing group several years ago that raised their own money for trips by collecting recyclables and turning them in for cash. Currently the local homeschooling group I am a member of has self-organized a set of baseball

teams using the dads and older teens as coaches.

Book Clubs
Again suitable for any age. You can tailor your selections to fit the needs of the group of children. My children attended one based upon the series Junior Great Books for a year and loved it.

Constitution Study
An enterprising mother ordered copies of the Constitution off the internet and started a study group reading and discussing the Constitution line by line. You would be surprised how much you can learn.

Public Speaking
One homeschooling mother I know was very involved in Toastmasters as an adult and wanted her children to have the experience as well. She started a public speaking club *(www.homeschoolspeakingclub.com)* that has been wildly successful.

Gardening
Find a mother who has a green thumb and rope her in for this one. Each child could do their own garden or the group could tend one together as they learn about gardening.

Appendix C

Homeschooling Organizations

Any list of state wide homeschooling organizations would be out of date by the time you were reading it. More and more are popping up and some are fizzling just as fast as I can type. So I have listed several internet resources where you can go to find the most recent information possible about the organizations available for you.

HSLDA (Home School Legal Defense Association)
This organization maintains a state-by-state listing of laws and organizations. They also have a wealth of other information available on the website and to their members. They are the only organization I know of that can provide an experienced level of legal support to homeschoolers. *www.hslda.org*

HomeSchool World
A great website that lists organizations, both state and local. They also list homeschooling conventions, curriculum resources, and they publish the Practical Homeschooling Magazine. *www.home-school.com*

Homeschool Central
A comprehensive website with information about national, state, and regional homeschooling groups as well as message boards and homeschool blogs. *www.homeschoolcentral.com*

Appendix D

Sample Homeschooling Letter

This is a sample of a letter that can be included with applications. You can modify it to suit your needs, and obviously it should reflect your unique homeschooling style and the accomplishments of your child. Note that it provides a background for homeschooling, explanation of the philosophy and courses taught, and a complete picture of the homeschooled child.

Dear _____ ,

Thank you for considering the application of our son/daughter, _____ , for admission to _____ . My husband and I are very excited about this opportunity for _____ , as we feel he/she will benefit greatly from the environment and academic excellence that _____ has achieved.

As I am sure you are aware after perusing his/her application, _____ is homeschooled, having never been in a traditional classroom setting. At an early age, it became evident that _____ would need more than a traditional classroom could offer in order to reach his/her full potential.

Our goals for homeschooling _____ included instilling a love of learning and a passion for the pursuit of knowledge. We stress a comprehensive understanding of the world and the complex interaction between subjects of study. Education is never labeled, boxed, and categorized separately, but rather intertwined so that relationships can be seen between disciplines.

This philosophy of education has directed the structure of _____ 's homeschooling experience. His/her subjects are organized with relationships in mind; e.g. ancient history was correlated with ancient literature and art while chemistry and biology were concomitantly introduced so that chemical processes in biological organisms could be understood. We don't confine or segregate learning according to time of day or day of week and many times lessons are taught seven days a week. Teachable moments are sought after and valued, and this often leads in a widely divergent track from the course being taught. An example of this occurred recently when studying the geography of Tanzania and Mt. Kilimanjaro. We broke from our geography studies to read Ernest Hemingway's short story, "The Snows of Kilimanjaro".

Teaching in our household is accomplished with a variety of materials. We rely heavily on written materials such as biographies, historical fiction, and works of literature, and we supplement these with textbooks as a reference source. Multimedia materials are used extensively; these include historical documentaries, scientific programs, and audiobooks. An example of this is when we incorporated PBS's series *The Elegant Universe* by Brian Greene into our lessons on physics.

Whenever possible, we incorporate first hand experiences – from travel and field trips, to visiting museums and performing arts shows – to reinforce the lessons and extend the learning opportunities. For example, when U.S. History was introduced, we took a trip to Jamestown, Williamsburg, Yorktown, Boston and several of the original capitals of the thirteen colonies. When ancient Egypt was being studied, we visited the Ramses II exhibition. Similarly, during _____'s human anatomy course, we combined the learning about major organ systems with a visit to the Body Worlds exhibit.

Both my husband and I see our role as facilitators rather than teachers. We encourage _____ to challenge assumptions and to engage in critical thinking and debate whenever possible. We have followed a mostly classical style of education, with many Charlotte Mason overtones. The early years focused on knowledge acquisition and included a wide variety of subjects combined with specific unit studies. As _____ grew older, this was refined to the study of a core course curriculum including mathematics, natural and physical sciences, world history and geography, logic, language arts (including literature, grammar, vocabulary, and composition), Latin, art, and music.

As _____ continued to mature, it became clear that he needed a more challenging academic environment. Because of his young age (eleven at the time), we researched local resources and decided to enroll him in an AP U.S. History course offered through the University of California Irvine's college preparatory program. This course consisted of materials regulated by the College Board and augmented by material presented by a professor from the UC system. _____ has done exceptionally well in this course, receiving an A (97%) in the first semester and currently with an A average (100%) in the second semester. Taking this into account, we have decided that he is ready to move to the next level of course work. _____ has clearly demonstrated that he is self-motivated and able to learn in the unstructured, minimally supervised online arena. He has never turned in an assignment late, has studied on his own without reminders, and has maintained a level of enthusiasm for learning with this course, even when the demands have been great upon him. Moreover, he has risen to the level of work required of the AP course without any diminution to his other coursework or extracurricular activities.

Apart from his academic success, _____ has shown himself to be truly exceptional in his varied extracurricular activities, and he has shown the ability to rise to any occasion or challenge thrown his way with grace and determination. This can most notably be seen in his Boy Scout experience, where he started in the Cub Scouts as a Tiger at age 5 and progressed through the ranks with enthusiasm. He was motivated to achieve even at an early age, earning his Arrow of Light and High Achiever Award as a Webelos II. When he bridged to Boy Scouts, he continued to set high goals for himself, reaching the rank of Star Scout by the age of 12 1/2, leaving only one more rank before achieving his objective of becoming an Eagle Scout.

_____ further embodies the Scout spirit in everything he does, from motivating and leading his troop to the Best Troop Award as an outing leader at the Emerald Bay Boy Scout Camp, to his receiving the Boy Scouts of America National Meritorious Award for Lifesaving.

This award was the result of _____ and a fellow scout being the first responders on the scene of a serious motorcycle accident in the Angeles National Forest while on their way to a camping trip. Without any regard to personal safety, he jumped out of the car, grabbed his first aid kit and rushed to the side of the cyclist to administer what first aid he could. Working in tandem with his fellow scout, _____ helped to coordinate the rescue effort and life flight of the motorcyclist, ultimately saving his life.

_____ has also shown the same level of tenacity in his other extracurricular activities. Last year he started his own business after he felt that science materials for homeschooled children were lacking. He wrote his own curriculum based on studying insects. It incorporated scientific concepts, such as the scientific method in his lessons. He created the product, determined the pricing, obtained materials and packaging, designed a website, and has successfully marketed the product for the past year. In many other aspects of his life, _____ has shown himself to be mature and responsible. When performing at violin recitals, his music teacher once remarked, "No matter how nervous he is, I can count on _____. He is rock solid."

_____ has a zest for life and communicates that to others in his friendly and outgoing personality. He loves the outdoors and enjoys participating in sporting activities such as scuba diving, sailing, snorkeling, kayaking, skiing, hiking, and backpacking. He especially likes to engage in learning new activities and skills.

In closing, we sincerely appreciate your consideration for _____'s admission and I truly believe that _____ will be able to succeed in the academic environment of _____ . If you have any questions, we would be happy to discuss them further with you or travel to meet with the admission office in person.

Sincerely,

_____

Notes

1 Unschooling is a term coined by the American educator John Holt, who championed the cause of allowing children to lead the direction of their education. Unschooling leads to a very individualized way of teaching as each child is allowed freedom to learn in their own way and at their own pace with the support of the parents.

2 Charlotte Mason was a British educator in the nineteenth century who developed a philosophy of education espousing a love of nature, living books, and narration. She also was one of the first to champion the importance of parental involvement in their children's education.

3 ERIC Identifier: ED395713
Publication Date: 1996-05-00
Author: Brophy, Jere
Source: ERIC Clearinghouse on Elementary and Early Childhood Education Urbana IL.

4 There is a wonderful series of books by E. D. Hirsch entitled *What Your* (1st, 2nd, etc.) *Grader Needs to Know* for each grade level of the elementary years. They are concise, easy to read, and very complete. They are also compatible with most state educational standards.

5 *National Geographic* has entire lesson plans on their website available to download for free.

6 Trade books in the publishing world are those that are intended for general readership, distributed to the general public through booksellers.

7 Visual Tracking Disorder is part of a spectrum of disabilities associated with the inability of the eyes to properly track across a page as a child is reading or the inability to maintain visual attention to a cue.

8 There is a lot of controversy about the accuracy of IQ testing. There have been studies that cite racial and ethnic biases inherent in the test structure. These are very real concerns but outside the scope of this book.

9 In case you are wondering, I ended up by making a test and giving it to the parents. They were able to decide whether they wanted to administer it or not. I graded the two that I got back; the others declined to take it. In my case, I gave the test to my daughter but not my son. This just goes to show how much individuality homeschooling allows, even within the same family.

References

Andreola, Karen. *A Charlotte Mason Companion: Personal Reflections on the Gentle Art of Learning*. Elkton, MD.: Charlotte Mason Research & Supply, 1998.

Apollo 13. VHS. Directed by Ron Howard. United States: Universal Studios, 1995.

Becker, Kirk A. *History of the Stanford-Binet Intelligence Scales: Content and Psychometrics*. Stanford-Binet Intelligence Scales, Fifth Edition Assessment Service Bulletin No. 1, 2003.

Brophy, Jere E., Eric Clearinghouse on Elementary, and Education Early Childhood. *Enhancing Students' Socialization Key Elements*. Urbana, IL: ERIC Clearinghouse on Elementary and Early Childhood Education, University of Illinois, 1996.

Collom, E. *The Ins and Outs of Homeschooling: The Determinants of Parental Motivations and Student Achievement*. Educational Administration Abstracts 41, no. 1 (2006).

EyeCare America. *Vision Therapies for Learning Disabilities*. Last modified May 2007. http://www.eyecareamerica.org/eyecare/treatment/alternative-therapies/vision-therapies-learning-disabilities.cfm

Holt, John Caldwell, and Patrick Farenga. *Teach Your Own: The John Holt Book of Homeschooling*. Cambridge, MA: Perseus Pub., 2003.

Kranz, Gene. *Failure Is Not an Option: Mission Control from Mercury to Apollo 13 and Beyond*. New York: Simon & Schuster, 2000.

Lines, Patricia M. *Homeschooling Comes of Age*. Public Interest 140, no. 140 (2000): 74-85.

Lois, Jennifer. *Emotionally Layered Accounts: Homeschoolers' Justifications for Maternal Deviance*. Deviant Behavior 30, no. 2 (2009): 201-34.

Lovell, Jim, and Jeffrey Kluger. *Lost Moon: The Perilous Voyage of Apollo 13*. Boston: Houghton Mifflin, 1994.

National Education Association. *2008-09 Adequate Yearly Progress (AYP) Results: Many More Schools Fail in Most States*. Accessed October 20, 2009. http://www. nea.org/home/16107.htm

Neufeldt, Victoria. *Webster's New World Dictionary: 4th College Edition*. [S.l.]: Macmillan, 1999.

Noelle, Scott. *The Daily Groove: How to Enjoy Parenting... Unconditionally!* Portland: CreateSpace, 2008.

Ray, Brian D. *Research Facts on Homeschooling*. National Home Education Research Institute. http://www.nheri.org/Research-Facts-on-Homeschooling. html.

Reich, Rob. *The Civic Perils of Homeschooling*. Educational Leadership 59, no. 7 (2002): 56-59.

Watson, Stephanie. *How Public School Works*. How Stuff Works.com. http:// people.howstuffworks.com/public-schools3.htm.

Willis, Mariaemma, and Victoria Kindle Hodson. *Discover Your Child's Learning Style: Children Learn in Unique Ways – Here's the Key to Every Child's Learning Success*. Rocklin, CA: Prima Pub., 1999.

Index

Index

About the Author

Bethany M. Gardiner, M.D. is a seasoned homeschooling mother with over a decade of experience in homeschooling her own children and teaching co-op classes for other homeschoolers. A National Merit Scholar who was accepted into the Honors Program at the University of Florida, she graduated in 1990 with a Bachelor's of Science in Mathematics and a Bachelor's of Arts in Statistics. Following graduation, she attended medical school at the University of Florida, graduating with honors in 1994. After completing medical school, Dr. Gardiner did her internship and residency at the University of Florida's Urban Campus, where she received the Resident Student Teacher Award. Upon completion of residency, she joined Interlachen Pediatrics in Orlando, FL. She is a board certified pediatrician and an internationally board certified lactation consultant. In addition to her homeschooling activities, Dr. Gardiner is very involved in volunteer work, including serving as a leader of her daughter's Girl Scout troop for the past seven years and a merit badge counselor for her son's Boy Scout troop. She also volunteered in the post Hurricane Katrina relief effort helping run the children's unit of a field hospital in Louisiana and working at a Red Cross shelter. Currently Dr. Gardiner lives in Utah, where she enjoys hiking, reading, needlework, and traveling, and is married to the same man she met as a freshman in college twenty-five years ago.